THE DIVE BAR QUALIFIER

A GUIDE FOR BETTER APPRECIATION OF
THE DIVE

TED MAGUIRE

Edited by Danielle Marston, @inkravens

Original photography by Ted Maguire unless otherwise noted.

Original Cover Art by Pamela Maguire

Original Spot Illustrations by Pamela Maguire, @pamlikesyou

This book was:

❀ Created with Vellum

To Pete Enos, (a.k.a. Angry Pete) great friend and true Dive Bar professional

CONTENTS

INTRODUCTION

Appreciation is in order.

A true Dive Bar deserves to be appreciated for a number of reasons. First off, they are the rebels of the service industry. Operating in the outskirts like a shunned child, still loved but considered different from the rest. They provide an opportunity for socializing that is unique and intensely real. Patrons give and receive a solid dose of entertaining comments and criticism more effectively than your average bar. They are the shelter for some who have trouble integrating. They do this starting earlier and ending later than most bars and all of that without a fake smile or other restaurant protocol happening daily at chains. They are real and deliver reality. Maybe you already love them or maybe you aren't quite sure what a Dive is. Either way there are a number of considerations and points to be made in order to fully appreciate this great subculture we call Dive Bars. Even if you are an expert on the subject, there are aspects presented here which may shed a different light and expand the reasons to cherish the Dive. For the novice, this information will become invaluable. We love to visit Dives and we think we know how to recognize them. The subjects presented here will help eliminate any doubt. After reading, you will know exactly what qualifies any bar as a Dive or not. If questioned, you will have specifics to back you up. This is important because there are people who are unaware of what truly makes a Dive Bar the thing of beauty that it is. These individuals run rampant in our society and get in the way of the real and true Dive experience we are seeking. They confuse the subject with ignorance, false narratives and pathetic viewpoints. The specifics presented here will help you defend against these Jackwagons. A real Dive should be appreciated but it's important to be armed with the focused knowledge of what makes these gems the special places we love. This book aims to clear the air of subjectivity and doubt. Even though opinion and local influence is at play, the information presented here is real and factual. Let's not get worked up just yet. You love Dive Bars and that is more important currently. After reading this book you might just love them even more.

With over 40 years experience in the restaurant industry, over 30 (and counting) years of that bartending at different establishments both divey and not, this author feels qualified enough to present this information with the kind of thoughtful insight and forthright conviction you can depend on. If Dive Bars are your passion then you are currently reading a book intended for you. If that's not enough, your opinions and comments can be submitted for review at (www.DiveBarBook.com).

1

IT'S A CONUNDRUM

One person's dreadful is another's nirvana

WHAT IS YOUR FAVORITE DIVE BAR?

You might have more than one. Your favorite could be a place you never admit going to because of it's bad reputation. Sometimes you just want a drink in a place where no one asks questions and the beers are cold, a real drinker's bar. Someone might suggest a place they frequent, *"Oh I love Pete's Lounge. That place is really divey!"* In quiet disagreement you think they have no idea what they're talking about. The place they mentioned isn't a Dive at all. You shake your head in disgust and walk off. Good job, you snubbed that Jackwagon while keeping your favorite spot a secret. You don't need ignorance like that hanging out at your place of sanctity. They would never appreciate a real Dive Bar anyway.

So what exactly is a Dive Bar? You know the answer but when you stop to think about it you realize the subject is more complex, no simple black and white definition. *"Oh, it's the kind of place you would never take your mother to."* Yes, but what if your mother is cool and enjoys a casual glass of cheap Chablis down at the Haunt. She might even know some of the regulars there. You say Dive, someone else says no, it's too clean to be a Dive. All of the sudden the question Dive or Not seems completely subjective even though we're all confident we know what the answer is.

"OH COME ON", you say. *"A dive has rough customers, it's dark, a biker bar kind of place."* Yes but what if they also have great food?

Really good, fresh seafood prepared by a talented chef that just happens to work there, then what. The place is known as a Biker Bar but they have great food. This back and forth can cause problems. People debate over this subject or worse, they make the wrong call and further spread ignorance. One thing people seem to agree on is that they love a great Dive. If you like to visit bars generally, then you probably have a Dive Bar you hold near and dear to your heart. Might be a place you only visit on occasion but you love it. You love it for all the wrong reasons and you love it enough that you will defend it. *"I know what a Dive Bar is and that place is definitely a DIVE BAR!"*

You feel as though it has earned this status and you are there to help maintain it's lowbrow level. The good news is you are probably correct but it's important to know more precisely what makes this bar a Dive. Even if no one questions the bar's status, you are someone who appreciates a Dive. Having better knowledge will help improve your overall experience of the Dive Bar subculture.

Scallop boat Capt. Lee personally brings his fresh scallops to this bar. Then he enjoys a beer. Some might consider this bar a Dive but should we?

Dive Bars are like an old sweater, comfortable but might have an odd smell. They are like a mad lover. The sex is great but you don't want to be seen with them in public. Maybe you love Dives because everyone there is just as messed up as you are. The more you discuss this, the more you discover a multitude of reasons why people love them. There seems to be no end, an unconditional, bottomless love for the Dive Bar.

Dives do not target a particular clientele of any kind. If you have money and would like a drink then by all means get in there. Men, women, tradesmen, medical professionals, people in business suits, bikers in leather, indigent or billionaire, everyone feels welcome and a real Dive will attract them all. On your first visit you might be met with leery eyed resistance but if you play your cards right you will soon be treated like family. Dives of all levels hit these basic points. The run-down quirkiness, need of little maintenance, the character of the room and the characters in it are all reasons we love Dives. They are usually known for pouring a stiff drink unless you are a regular customer in which case the drink could be substantially lethal. Service is usually delivered with little or no speaking except maybe a *"How ya been"* or *"You're kinda late tonight."* Often bartenders know customers so well that drinks are made before they even open the door. Bartenders inadvertently know their patrons' habits. This sort of knowledge can be a curse for restaurant staff. Knowing less is better sometimes.

DIVE BARS ARE CREATED over time in an organic way that is neither forced nor deliberately built. This point cannot be stressed enough. Hold on, that statement needs to be emphasized. Dive Bars are created over time in an organic way that is neither forced nor deliberately built. If a new bar opens and is called a "Dive" on day one, this is a mistake. The important but basic elements of a Dive have not been given a chance to take place. The new bar might eventually get there but it must experience some wear and tear over time. An eclectic owner needs to influence the character of the room. Dust needs to build up in the corners, a neglected leaky roof might leave a permanent stain down the wall, maybe a lousy patch job from an angry fist into drywall, regardless one is not called a Senior Citizen on the day they are born. One must live a little and a real Dive has lived a lot. The good ones have been around for decades, not new in any sense. Remember it cannot be deliberately created. It must evolve into a divey situation over time. If you are looking to own one your only option is to buy it currently in operation, then keep it divey. This is rare because of the business risks. Imagine someone buying a business that appears tired and run-down. This new buyer will most likely clean it up and generally improve things. Yet another reason we must appreciate Dives. They can easily be cleaned up and thus disappear. Is there such a thing as a clean Dive Bar with a new coat of paint, complete with air fresheners in the restroom? You get the point.

INTERESTINGLY, if a Dive Bar can just be cleaned up and become less divey then why don't owners do that? If you own a business and it's considered dirty and badly run then why aren't changes made? In the back of our minds, we know better. We know that the owner could simply enforce a higher standard but that doesn't happen. We find a certain amusement in this. A certain appreciation for the owner's rebel attitude perhaps. Maybe it's just their complete disregard for normal business practices that makes us appreciate the situation in an entertaining way. Besides, people still patronize even though it's considered derelict. Not only do they patronize, they love the place as if it's their child and give this place the pet name *Dive Bar*.

AN INDIVIDUAL's passion can cause heated debates or even outright arguments and shoving, (no violence please.) Once you understand the information presented here, you will better grasp the overall concept of a Dive Bar and ultimately have an improved position for future discussions, which will most definitely happen. Simple consideration of what a real Dive should be along with scoring basic features about the establishment will give you a better standpoint, and thus, help you determine if the bar in question is actually a Dive and to what level.   Keep this in mind as we delve into the seedy, run-down-filthy yet beautiful, amazing and lovable world of Dive Bars.

Who came up with this nonsense anyway?

It's in books, text, wikipedia, conversations and more. Statements about Dive Bars using words like disreputable, sinister and a place of ill repute used in various definitions throughout the decades.   An important consideration is that the term Dive Bar seems to be specific to North America.   An edition of the Oxford English Dictionary says that in the United States in the 1880's the term Dive Bar referred to an illegal drinking den or other place of ill repute, especially one located in a basement. By the time Prohibition took place in the 1920's, people were accustomed to keeping their booze under wraps, so diving into a basement wasn't a bad idea.   One could argue that Dives are all over the world and they'd be correct.   However, using the term "Dive Bar" to describe a particular type of establishment seems basically a North American thing.   Equally important is that we need a standard to judge the Dive against (it seems we're judgy.)

There needs to be a nice, fresh, smiley bar in the back of our minds in order for us to realize the difference. This may seem ridiculous to point out but the term Dive Bar would never have been coined if there wasn't a higher standard of establishments to compare with.   For example many bars in Mexico or the Caribbean could be considered Dives from the average tourist's point of view.   This judgement is incorrect because local laws and standards allow for businesses to operate in drastic contrast to the average liquor licensing and laws of operation in mainland United States. One should not call the Michelada Stand a Dive even if it's the seediest bar you've ever been to. Besides they probably make the best Michelada you'll ever taste which means they're not so divey. That said, Dive Bars definitely exist in the United States and Canada, it is arguable whether the term is used outside these countries. An individual from the Netherlands referred to this kind of bar as a "Neighborhood Bar" while another from Ireland had heard the term Dive Bar and said, "We just call them a Shit Hole."

SO THOSE IN NORTH AMERICA, should take great pride in owning the origins and usage of the term Dive Bar. Interestingly, people worldwide will stop for refreshment and seek out the seediest of places to do so. If you find yourself in a place where the vast majority of bars are seedy and derelict then it's likely the locals do not call them Dive Bars. These utopian places do exist. Be careful never to insult locals. Your perspective may be vastly different from theirs so be sure not to inadvertently step on toes by throwing around the term Dive Bar, even while you're in Northern Wisconsin where the term seemingly originated, (kudos to Northern Wisconsin.)

Ok, we're being judgy but not in a bad way. However, if a person incorrectly labels a bar divey when it's not, this is bad. This could cause a number of problems. A small pub with decent food and relatively clean appearance does not say Dive right? Then why did some Jackwagon just refer to the place as a Dive? This person is abusing the term and making uneducated statements which could end up insulting others, not to mention they are missing out on the real experience. This is not good on many levels but most importantly they are missing out. They were at a bar, they thought it was a Dive so now they feel accomplished. In reality they have cheated themselves out of the real Dive experience by incorrectly identifying the place. They have accomplished nothing except visiting a restaurant. Unfortunately, this individual will continue their misguided trajectory until better informed. The specific points and information contained here are intended to help the reader make better and more accurate determinations. No one wants to be *that guy*. The guy who sends people on ill-conceived missions, recommending a friendly family restaurant they think is a great Dive. We should all do our best to avoid Jackwagonry.

Five General Categories to keep in mind
1. Location (physical address and things outside)
2. Inside Decor and Such (things inside and the structure itself)
3. The Character of the room and the Characters hanging out, (Owner, Staff, Regulars and the overall mood)
4. Restrooms (this could be a book in itself)
5. Singularities (things about a bar that are unique and help affirm you are at a Dive)

EACH CATEGORY HAS important aspects and nuances for consideration. The chapters following will break these down and provide real examples, experiences and anecdotes intended to help you better identify these specific elements. You may think a bar is a great Dive until you consider more of these points. Your opinion might sway one way or another. Maybe your favorite Dive is even more divey than you realized. Now wouldn't that be amazing.

2

LOCATION

Off the beaten path or right under your nose

GENERALLY A DIVE BAR WILL NOT BE LOCATED IN A HIGH-RENT district but one never knows. If the address of the bar is in a nice neighborhood then something else is probably messed up. For example the bar itself looks like an old garden shed. Snake & Jake's Christmas Club Lounge in New Orleans is a truly amazing example of this.

*Snake & Jake's Christmas Club Lounge, New Orleans,
LA*

Located in the middle of an affluent neighborhood, the bar
seems out of place. Homes next door are valued at half a million
plus. As you approach for the first time you think you're on the
wrong street. Then, like a glorious sunrise, there she is. Her
wonderful state of ramshackle neglect makes you overwhelmed
with anticipation. You feel like a kid about to enter the gates at
Disney World. *"Hurry, let's get in there before the building
collapses, we must have a cold Schlitz, Oh the humanity!"*
Scenarios like this add to the bar's potential Dive Level. This is
a perfect example of the "Unexpected Location" Dive Points,
(described in detail later.) These rare gems are so beautiful we
never want them to go away. Hopefully the millionaire next
door appreciates a neighbor like Snake & Jake's.

THE BEACH BAR, Tiki Hut, Island Paradise sort of place is
confusing to many people because these bars are extremely casual. Some look at a Tiki Hut and want to call it a Dive Bar but
this is where you need to stick closely to Maguire's Dive Bar
Qualification System and be as unbiased as possible when scoring. A beach, lakefront or island destination almost always says
you are not in Dive country even if other elements indicate you
are. There are exceptions but consider this, you are on the

beach. Ok there's loud customers, drinks are strong, eclectic decor and weird signage, the list goes on in support of a Dive BUT you are on the beach. A beautiful view of any kind almost always disqualifies the bar as a Dive. Additionally Beach Bars often have good food. Some of the best seafood you can get is at places near the water, not exactly divey right?

LE TUB SALOON IN HOLLYWOOD, Florida might be an exception to this. Located on the intracoastal, the place is loaded with Dive fundamentals such as toilet bowl planters, wonderfully rustic decor and a maze-like floor plan just to get to the restroom. Le Tub is well known for a Giant Burger which you can enjoy while million dollar boats pass gracefully through the waterway. There are characteristics on both sides of the Dive discussion. Considering all the criteria is important for an accurate assessment. You badly want to qualify the bar as a Dive. There are so many lovable, messed up aspects but just look at the view. What a beautiful view you have right from your barstool looking out over the water as majestic sailboats pass by. If you have accounted for everything on the Dive Points List, the numbers do not lie. Achieving Dive Status should not be handed out freely. The status is earned and should be appreciated but only if it's genuine. The real Dives, struggling in messed up situations, are depending on all of us to make sound determinations. Just because you swam up to a beach bar, made your own drink because there's no staff, paid via the honor system at a Tiki Hut in complete disrepair does not mean you are at a Dive Bar. It sounds like you're at a really cool beach bar somewhere in the Caribbean. The folks back at Gooski's in Pittsburgh might take offense when you call that Tiki Hut a Dive Bar. Can we please make correct, intelligent and sound judgments on the subject of Dive Bars, thank you.

Real Estate values greatly affect businesses and might be the largest contributor to a Dive closing its doors next to the owner making bad decisions. A Dive Bar in a high rent district might just be looking for the right buyer and will soon become history. Naturally businesses prefer locations with lots of traffic. You might find a Dive in a high traffic area but most likely the Real Estate values there are too high for one to make a go of it. Are there any Dives on 5th Avenue in Manhattan or is it just a casual bar considered a Dive by Manhattan standards. If the property values become high enough this changes the business equation. Owners sell the property and move on and no one blames them but we do miss their bars.

ONE EXAMPLE of this could be The Gurnet Inn, not always thought of as a Dive because the building stood on the sea wall, Duxbury Beach in Massachusetts. Due to catastrophic storm damage only part of the building was salvaged and luckily that part included the lounge. Over time a more dive-like situation developed. During the last several seasons of the "Gurnet" the bar would still open in summer months, (the original Inn had long since closed.) They served cocktails in small round glasses about the size of a baseball, flat on the bottom. These vintage little glasses added to the bar's potential Dive Point total. They were something you might have drank from as a child visiting your grandmother. The bartender would make your cocktail with a touch of contempt and then return to cutting straws in half with scissors. Un-cut straws were too long for the little round glassware. This might explain the bartender's surly demeanor (also

Dive Points.) Anyone having to cut all the straws in half should be given a pass on the friendly service thing. Amazingly there were no real views of the ocean or beach even though the lounge was mere feet from the sand and surf. The bar itself was on the opposing side and faced away towards the street. Any nice views would have been enjoyed by guests of the inn had that side still been operating. This "No view of the ocean" also added to a potential Dive status because it didn't make sense. Imagine owning a bar with beautiful ocean views but your customers can't really see any of it. Hey, just drink your beer and shut up, no need for views, you simmah down with that view nonsense... you.

Ultimately the building was demolished and a beautiful multi-million dollar residence now occupies that address on the sea wall. As much as folks miss the old Gurnet Inn, one cannot blame the family for taking this action. Would you rather operate a seasonal bar, cutting straws in half or sell and take your millions. In other words, *"Back in the day, there was this bar there. It was great, we miss it."* Yet another reason to get out and visit these unique little spots before they disappear.

OKAY SO NOW YOU are at a less desirable location. It's not exactly "Off the beaten path" but at least it's not waterfront. Great, what else about the location might help qualify Dive Status. Let's see... located directly behind the bar is a junkyard. Wait what, a junkyard? That's amazing.

A pleasant "Junkyard Setting" behind the bar

How about railroad tracks or a situation where customers have to walk behind a bus station, perfect. Ideally the location should be undesirable in some way or perhaps make you look around before you park your car.

THERE MIGHT BE a vacant storefront next door. Yes, vacancies, amazing. Or perhaps a shop that supports the customers of the bar. These support businesses sell things that may not be available from the bar directly such as tobacco/lottery/Check Cashing kind of services, convenience store items, etc. A pizza/sub shop might be located nearby because a real Dive offers no food. Occasionally Dive patrons might want something besides Slim Jims or peanuts though we can't imagine why. Support businesses can be considered part of a Dive business community if you will. However, if the bar sells its own lottery, scratch tickets, KENO etc. this means additional Dive Points. Consider the favorable, negative aspects. If the location makes you say, *"This looks good and seedy"*, then you are on the right track. A location where the average business might avoid or would deter customers from stopping is where a Dive Bar feels at home. Imagine a bunch of regulars sipping a refreshing barley soda in the darkness, their faces lit only by the KENO screen while outside it's a beautiful, sunny day. Sounds like we got ourselves a Dive Bar.

WHEN VISITING A NEW AREA, asking locals where to find a Dive Bar in their community will be met with varied reactions. You will need to take into account who you are talking to and then interpret the answer. Asking the senior citizen who volunteers at the Visitor's Center is not recommended. On the other hand the 23 year old bartender at the sports bar might not know what the term "Dive Bar" means. Try being more specific. Your online search suggested a place. If you want to get a local opinion you could ask, for example, *"What do you think of that bar, Carmine's Villa?"* If the 23 year old says, *"Oh that place is nasty, it's all old people."* then Carmine's might actually be a great Dive. The person at the Visitor's Center might say, *"I'm not familiar with that place but you could try Sam's, they have great food."* You see neither individual recommended Carmine's but the place might be exactly what you're looking for. If they both recommended Carmine's then you cross it off your list of possible visits. A bar that appeals to both young, old and a visitor's center is most likely not going to be a Dive. There is only so much time, why waste it on sunshine, good food and smiling staff when you could be enjoying an ice cold Stroh's and some pickled eggs in the glorious gloom of Bill's Corner Bar.

Outer Appearance, Grounds & Entrance
Does the front of the building or entrance look inviting?

Perhaps there are flowers and plantings along a carefully pointed bluestone walkway from the valet desk. Is there attractive youthful staff with menus there to greet you? No? Alrighty then, how about a general sense of neglect and a pathway of cigarette butts and empty nip bottles. Now we're talking.

Hopefully the entrance will project the "Element of Fear." Not enough to make you run but if you are approaching the establishment for the first time and you are questioning your decision to enter, then you might be at a Dive Bar. This is a good thing. A novice will avoid, while a professional feels right at home. A professional might spend more time at their favorite bar than they spend at their own home. This is a fact we shall not speak of again.

THE DOOR or entryway at a dive bar should be odd or quirky in some way. Perhaps the entire building is as well. It's no one's fault necessarily. This is usually the result of many things such as poorly executed renovations or hack repair jobs or maybe because the original use of the building was not intended as a bar which explains why the building looks like a small residence.

"I've driven by this place a million times and never knew there was a bar here"

Dives are really good at appearing to be closed all of the time. Even if they're fully open, there simply isn't any other business that looks more closed than a good Dive Bar. *"It's FINE!,* (says the owner), *you don't need to turn on the outside lights, what are you thinking?!?"* A Dive owner is more apt to be entirely unaware that their bar looks closed all of the time. Additionally, there are customers who appreciate this "Closed Look" thing. It's counterintuitive to most businesses but some regulars prefer no disturbances while self-medicating. Chatting it up is not on their list, especially with a new, annoying happy person. A new, happy customer might screw up quiet paper reading time. For example, Happy Neil has stopped in for the first time. He thinks it's a good idea to strike up a conversation with Angry Pete. Angry is a regular sitting in his usual stool, reading the newspaper, (some still do this.) Neil asks, *"So what do you do for work?"* Pete turns to him slowly and replies, *"What do I do? I mind my own business. That's what I do!"*

In this instance, looking closed would have been helpful to Happy Neil as he would have kept driving and avoided this confrontation.

Sometimes the front door is permanently locked. This is the door that rookies try to open unsuccessfully. There's usually a faded sign on that door telling folks to use a different entrance. You know the sign. It's made with scrap plywood and a sharpie marker. It's the weathered sign you can sort of still read with an arrow pointing to use the other door around to the side. The real entrance will have a couple of people standing outside, enjoying tobacco while they watch people use the wrong door. If you happen to be the rookie in this case, don't worry. The regulars have already judged you. They may even have wagered on it. *"Five bucks says he goes to the wrong door."* It's too late, go inside anyhow. May as well have a drink.

IT'S OFTEN SAID that the number of motorcycles parked outside is a good indicator of a Dive Bar. *"There were like a hundred bikes, the place must be really divey."* The number of motorcycles visible outside a bar has no bearing on Dive Status. There are all sorts of bars and restaurants visited by bikers, divey and not. There are also many different types of bikers. Some are hardcore and ride daily while some only ride a few times a year. Sure there are great Dives associated with Bikers but as a rule, motorcycles parked outside, even in high numbers, doesn't necessarily mean Dive Bar. People tend to group Dives and

Bikers together. To make this more complicated Bikers do in fact hangout at Dives. Biker's are a solid part of the fabric in Dive Bar culture. That said, so are nurses, educators, tradesmen... everyone right? If you see a bunch of bikes parked outside it may or may not be a Dive. You will need to go in and patronize to get the real answer.

3

INSIDE DECOR & SUCH

I can't wait to see how he's decorated the place

YOU ENTER A BAR AND WHEN YOUR EYES FINALLY ADJUST TO THE darkness, you see the entire bar has turned to look at you. There's an odd smell, might be from the carpet that your shoes are sticking to. You have a flashback memory of your mother warning against these activities, don't worry it's just a Dive Bar. The good people of our society are all out hiking and enjoying the fresh air and sunshine while you have chosen dimly lit ambiance, state sponsored gambling and the slow insidious destruction of your liver.

Beautiful day outside but you have a better idea

Congratulations, you are a Dive Appreciateur. To say you are an enthusiast would be correct but the word *enthusiast* implies a hobby or something potentially lame. You know full well your Dive activity is a lifestyle. Nothing lame about it. No need to label it with words, just show up and patronize with honor. We call them Dive Bars. Being a Dive regular and appreciating these little gems of our world is as important as hiking or going to the museum, perhaps more important. These feelings are worth embracing with unwavering, resolute conviction.

AN AUTHENTIC DIVE has had time to evolve into the amazing wonder that you experience. An interesting collection of oddities, pictures, vintage advertising, various taxidermy and such, accumulated over the years. The best collections are those that seem never ending. You notice something new every time you go in. It makes you feel as if you have entered an eclectic antique picker's barn and thankfully they remembered to install a bar as well. The decor could be almost anything, and chances are someone will soon ask, *"Honestly Billy, where do you find this garbage?"* Billy the owner has been collecting things for years. Maybe an old Schlitz clock that no longer keeps time but its backlight shines the way to the restroom down an otherwise dark hallway. Appreciable dust should also be part of this collection.

Nothing like noticeable dust to lend a feeling of authenticity to any Dive Bar. One owner claimed to be furious with an employee for cleaning too much. Apparently the employee had polished several brass nautical fixtures at the bar. Wiping away decades of patina in seconds. This effort was met with *"Just stock the beers and get back to reading the paper for crying out loud!"* from the owner. A tough lesson for the employee but one must learn to appreciate years of dust and weathered oxidation of brass decor. The employee did in fact stock the beers but wasn't sure about reading the paper so naturally the cell phone came out instead. A generational disconnect maybe but it's great that a younger individual can find employment and be fostered in the ways of the Dive.

The Beer Fridge Sticker collection is always a fun thing.

These sticker collections also find themselves on doors or other places and provide hours of entertaining amusement. No one seems to know where this activity started but these sticker laden wonders seem to happen all over the country, looking like an old piece of luggage covered with travel stamps.

Slogans and punchlines, religious and political messages, ski mountains, craft breweries, no particular theme but always fun and reassuring that you are at a Dive. An older bar might have some great examples of Americana, a long expired political campaign, *"Vote McGovern"* or other sentiment of days past.

Sticker Collection greets customers at this watering hole

Novelties like this are great conversation pieces and usually have a story beyond the sticker itself. *"Ya Phillip had that sticker on his boat trailer for years. He had to take it off before he sold the boat, the guy said he wasn't going to buy it with that ridiculous sticker...".* So you see, Phil had a great idea to carefully preserve the sticker knowing that the bar would be a perfect place to continue its life and add some vintage novelty in the meantime. Who said Phil wasn't a genius.

HOUSE RULES and hand written signs are something else you might experience at Dives. These are temporary paper signs which establish rules of some sort like "No dancing on the tables" or "Do not order food from the kitchen."

Whatever you do, don't order food! At least not from that kitchen anyway.

THESE SIGNS ARE NOT INTENDED to be humorous but ultimately they beg the question, What sort of activities go on in this establishment that requires a sign like this? Makes you think you missed out on a crazy night of shenanigans that lead to a quick employee meeting the next day. *"Ok everyone, Mary is going to write up a sign so this doesn't happen again..."*. Mary does this knowing it's entirely futile. She will be shaking her head as she tapes the paper to the wall hoping at least some of the customers read and understand the issue. One establishment went as far posting a complete list of rules they call the "Bar Code of Conduct".

Just having this list posted should be more than enough for you to love the place. The list suggests behavior that would be considered very normal by most standards. However, the management needed to inform their regulars to act more like normal people. A lovely example that speaks of Dive wonderment. The list also includes penalties, a one, two, three strikes you're out scenario. Remember being barred from your favorite Dive is a penalty worse than death. The banned individual feels lost and has terrible separation anxiety. It's an effective tool in keeping the peace and/or protecting the tables from snapping in half from the weight of dancers.

Yahtzee dice rolling is at many bars but Dive bars for sure. If you're not a regular you might pass on playing. This is the game where you bet a few dollars and try to roll 5 of a kind. If you decide to roll and you win, it is customary to buy everyone a drink (or two) and over-tip the bartender. It's your judgment but keep in mind the money in the pot is all from the regulars. If you are not a regular and you won all their money you might consider buying a round and over-tipping. This should be done every time someone wins the Yahtzee money, regular customer or not. If you don't understand what is being said here, it's best not to play this game.

IMPROVEMENTS AT DIVES are made in the most creative manner. *"Hey Jimmy, we can add another pool table upfront if we change the entrance and have people come around the side door instead, wadda ya think?"* Dive Bar owners are at the forefront when it comes to these innovative improvement ideas.

"Just built the new wall so it comes right up to the window ok, that'll be good. And leave enough room so we can keep extra toilet paper on the sill there, you know what I'm saying"

It's part of the charm that develops over time in a Dive. At the point when improvements are being considered, no one will stop to think about practical things like the flow of foot traffic or even the local building codes and fire ordinance regulations, but that's ok because the Building Inspector is a regular. So when *Jimmy* asked him about these improvement ideas, the inspector just shook his head and looked down at his beer in exhausted disbelief.

THE GREAT THING about repairs and renovations at a Dive is that the Tradesman who does the work is usually a regular and now must stand the criticism and abuse from his fellow Tradesmen who are also regulars and now feel free to judge the work even though they couldn't be bothered to do the job themselves.

"Bobby, you hung the door like a blind man. Look at this garbage. My apprentice kid does better work." During the holidays, Bobby will receive a bunch of eyeglasses as joke gifts so he can *"See what he's doing next time,"* tough love at a dive for sure.

AS FAR AS Dives are concerned, the word renovations is used very loosely. Many owners choose the minimal approach which is perfectly acceptable. Let's face it if a Dive owner starts throwing lots of money at grandiose plans to renovate then regulars should be concerned. Their Dive might be in jeopardy, cleaned up too much and disappear. No need to improve things too much after all. The floor at the Old Colony Tap in Provincetown, Massachusetts is a great example of the minimal approach.

Well seasoned bar-top

Beautifully preserved floor at the O.C.

If patrons cannot properly negotiate walking on this then they could very well get shut off. Albeit uneven, the floor does get maintained. The individual who refinished that floor did a great job. Just look at how the sunshine gleams off the well seasoned, wood surface. Unfortunately the individual who did that work was shut off anyhow, (more details in the next chapter.)

COCKTAILS OFFERINGS

Basic mixed drinks like Vodka-Soda or Rum & Coke are standard offerings which do not affect your assessment one way or another. That said, the type of drinks a bar makes can affect its Dive Status, maybe even to the degree that the bar should not be considered a Dive at all. For example, Craft Cocktails. If the bar offers these you are NOT in a Dive. These drinks are the Prohibition Era, multi step procedure, specialty ingredients not widely available, typically priced above average, etc. Examples include the Sazerac, Old Fashioned, Negroni, Ramos Gin Fizz, Moscow Mule (especially if served in the traditional copper mug), Mojito, Mint Julep, Sidecar, Ward 8, French 75, Muddled anything (Dives are not known for muddling), Organic ingredients, drinks with bitters, especially if the bitters is other than Angostura, the list goes on. Craft Cocktails pretty much disqualify a bar as a Dive because these sorts of cocktails go against Dive ethics. This may be an unwritten rule but well…
you just read it.

THE MARTINI and Manhattan are two cocktails often mistakenly lumped in with the Craft Cocktail group. If prepared a certain way they can be considered a Craft Cocktail. However, even the dirtiest Dives might make you a Martini or Manhattan without issue. Most likely there is a regular that loves a V.O. Manhattan and the Dive will have the ingredients on hand for that. So, if the bar seems like a great Dive but someone just ordered a

Manhattan, no worries. On the other hand if the customer orders a Ramos Gin Fizz and the bartender starts shaking one up then you are not in a Dive. If you are unsure, simply ask the bartender if they have a Drink Menu. The answer should determine everything. If you are handed a printed cocktail menu you can simply read the kind of ingredients available BUT you don't even need to do that. A printed drink menu itself says you are not at a Dive. On the other hand if you ask for the drink menu and the bartender looks at you like you are nuts, you might be at a Dive. Order a bottle of beer, a nationally recognized label please, don't further distance yourself by asking for a bottle of a little known brewery in nowhere, Fly-Over State, I'm sure it's a great beer but...

HOUSE SPECIALTY VERSUS THE "MYSTERY SHOT", don't get confused. House Specialty might be a rum drink for example, known for its alcoholic strength and has a creative name like "Killa McGilla" or something. The "Goombay Smash" is a tasty rum drink that helped put the Wellfleet Beachcomber on the map but it is not considered a Craft Cocktail nor does it carry Dive points.

Signage inside "The Comber"

Additionally the Beachcomber is not a Dive Bar (an amazing view from the 60 foot bluff looking out over the Atlantic Ocean pretty much disqualifies Dive Status.) Specialty or House drinks similar to the Goombay Smash are common at many establishments, divey and not. The "Mystery Shot" is different however. Dives are famous for the Mystery Shot. Dive culture may have in fact created this phenomena. Almost every Dive sells a version of one. The Quarterdeck Lounge in Hyannis, MA is well known for the "QD Shot". The recipe is not public knowledge but might include whatever sample bottle the liquor distributor has provided to the bar for a dollar, usually a flavored vodka but rest assured it's nothing fancy, the bartender mixes a batch of it in advance so the recipe might be two bottles, add a can of Redbull and some powdered red drink mix, stir. The bar then doubles down by offering a Pabst Blue Ribbon draft with the "QD Shot" all for 5 bucks. The shot together with the PBR is unofficially-officially known as a "Happy Meal".

"Happy Meal" at the QD

Some regulars order this lovely combo by politely asking the bartender for "Boaf". Asking for "Boaf" will not only get you two delicious beverages at a great price but it also indicates you are *with* the house and not *againit*. To recap, the House Specialty, Killa McGilla rum punch is not divey while the "Mystery Shot" is solidly Dive Bar culture.

If the house drink includes less expensive ingredients and is mixed using the special "Mystery Shot" batch method then you should apply Dive Points.

Mmmm yes, it's a mystery...

If you ask the bartender for a *"vodka-soda please"* and the bartender looks at you sideways and says, *"MIXED*

DRINKS???" then you might consider politely changing your order to a basic bottled beer. Secondly, you need to realize you are probably at a great Dive Bar so calmly pay attention. The vodka-soda, rum & coke, gin & tonic, etc. are all basic cocktails which any bar should be able to make easily. If you order one and there seems to be confusion, this is okay, just switch to your Backup Beverage and you're all set. The push-back you got by ordering a mixed drink could mean any number of things so re-ordering a simple beer gives everyone a second to evaluate the situation. Carolyn's Lounge in Houma, Louisiana is an amazing bar where you're sure to find Dive Points.

Carolyn's Lounge on Bayou Cane, Houma, LA

The Bartender there was very accommodating and was able to make the requested vodka-soda with some interpretation. He may have just been filling in for a few hours, not exactly sure. Part of the situation, however, is that the word "Soda" has different meanings around the country. "Soda" in many places is short for soda-water, also called seltzer by many or to some it might be a Coke or Pepsi, might even be orange or grape flavor. Keep in mind the local terminology might be different from your own.

· · ·

To make things more complicated, local influences definitely affect Dive status. Some people call Dives "Blue Collar Bars". Carolyn's Lounge was described by a girl in her early 20's as an "Old People's Bar." However, the customers at Carolyn's averaged 40, not exactly old. Additionally, it's likely that no one at Carolyn's would have called it a Dive because they are all accustomed to casual sort of places. The point is the definition of Dive Bar changes somewhat with local influences. The material presented in this book is intended to provide a path for clarity. Specific aspects to consider. With specifics, you can make a more concrete determination, right? Either way it's important to be aware that not everyone will understand this Dive concept so tread lightly out there especially when you are not the local. Maguire's Dive Bar Qualifier is a system that was created with careful consideration of the varying circumstances. It is not perfect (wait yes it is) but if followed carefully it should provide you with a solid determination regarding any bar in question.

4

THE CHARACTERS

The people make the show

A BAR OWNER'S PERSONALITY CAN GREATLY AFFECT THEIR employees but for survival purposes, the owner of a Dive Bar should be someone full of personality and plenty of self confidence. Thankfully, they own a bar where their personality thrives and shines like the morning dew glistening on the side of an overstuffed dumpster waiting to be emptied. A side effect of one owner's personality seems to have caused garbage to be piled high until the bill dispute is resolved with the trash company. This owner, you see, has an ongoing condition when paying certain bills and the staff is then left to deal with the situation. The staff was instructed to leave nothing outside of the dumpster at the end of the day. No uncertain terms, all the trash must be in the dumpster. So they carefully placed trash bags creating a mounded heap much higher than the dumpster itself. They congratulated Kyle who was able to toss the last bag of trash high enough to remain on top and not slide back off for someone else to attempt. Playing an impromptu game of trash bag madness. The late night competition was fierce, swinging trash bags like an Olympian swings the Hammer high into the air. Everyone cheering as they finish their last shifties before heading home for the night. *"You did it Kyle, Great Job!"* They knew the owner would have cursed them the next day had any bags been left on the ground outside of the dumpster. None of them wanted to be the cause of such a travesty.

A Dive owner who's been working for decades will hopefully have established a beautiful mess over time. Almost a miniature museum of strange collectables begging for their story to be told. The purchase of a new living room set for their home provides an opportunity to graciously donate the old set to the bar. There is really nothing better than Phil's old couch and matching loveseat to furbish his establishment. Already messed up so no worries for the shaky handed beverage. In other cases a beloved owner has passed away and thankfully the new owner had some sensibility to continue the charm. Keeping most things in place, only making minor changes. They bought a Dive, so a Dive it shall remain. An owner with this kind of sensibility and foresight should be revered as a genius. This individual knew that decades of dust settled on the place and created a particular environment that cannot easily be duplicated.

Various collectables and suggestive art

IN SOME CASES the owner has been bailed out of debt and allowed to continue in place. This might be rare but the generosity of some can be a beautiful thing. Examples of generosity are amazing when you discover them. Dive Bars might be the last place you'd expect to come across this but people pay it forward, even at Dives.

SOMETIMES THERE ARE two owners who, for the life of them, can't seem to agree on anything so nothing happens or the wrong thing happens. Over time a bar can become wonderfully divey given this scenario. Let's say the front needs to be painted but the owners cannot agree on what color, the budget, who is going to do the work, etc. so the project gets delayed... and delayed. Soon the front starts looking like an abandoned shack. Apply that scenario to the rest of their business, add in some time and voila, you have yourself a Dive Bar. It's not what the owners had in mind but their procrastination should be recognized as an achievement in Can-Do delayishment. Besides the customers still come in and seem to love it saying, the peeling paint gives the place personality. *"Don't change a thing."* Knowing full well that's going to happen.

WHEN DISCUSSING specifics about a bar's character it can be difficult to single out one criteria without involving another. Usually owners and their bars are direct reflections of each other. Some of the attributes overlap. An undesirable location for example, begs the question, why would someone put a bar there? Then you meet the owner, this person is completely unique and has been a life-long risk taker so the crazy location becomes more understandable. The owner and staff help create the bar's personality whether intended or not. Then add in customers who are begging to become part of the madness and with any luck a "Healthy Dive" will be firmly in place. A community of intemperate personalities acting subtly disobedient while self medicating in a location, which by many, is viewed as downright filthy or worse. This kind of character is not good, it's GREAT. The potential for down to Earth, real people being themselves in a place where everyone is comfortable presents itself better than ever. The release and escape from the pressures of life is more apt to occur. There will be some who act so ridiculous that the others feel better about themselves after witnessing. They are similar to a class clown in a more grown-up setting, confident to continue a downward spiral into the abyss, knowing someone at their Dive will offer a hand and pull them back before it's too late. If people judge you it doesn't matter because at a Dive, sooner or later someone or something else will take the limelight away from you. Let's face it, where else can a woman in her late 70s act completely certifiable, stand up on her bar stool, screaming profanity as she hikes up her skirt, flashing the TV because her hockey team has just lost. The bartender who had a front row seat to this display, politely asks her to sit down. Her indignant response, *"Oh it's okay, I'm wearing pantyhose."* Thankfully that bartender has since recovered.

THE RESTAURANT INDUSTRY is in continuous flux and Dive Bars are no exception to this. Some of the elements that define a Dive are the same things that cause a business to fail and close. Several months of an owner's neglect can cause a bar to seem like a Dive even if it's not. For example, the current owner bought a bar because they always wanted to own one. The ugly truth is that they had no idea how consuming the business was going to be. Over time they have grown completely exhausted by it. They are trying to sell it, (maybe desperately) while spending as little as possible before they unload this bar they always wanted. A sale could take time and during this period the establishment could become rundown, regular cleaning drops off, stock of food and booze are low or out. This may seem like a Dive but it's not. It's suggested you offer sympathy to the outgoing owner because they probably lost their shirt in all this mess.

IF A RESTAURANT or bar closes there might be some sell off of equipment. A savvy owner is always on the look-out for this opportunity. After all, they might need something for their own bar. The "Pack Rat Owner" however, takes things to a different level. This person buys things so often that the staff is always on guard. This owner will have a garage at home full to the top, hoarder style. It might sound great to have a couple of backup beer coolers but only if they work properly. It's a huge project swapping out a cooler only to find out you need to do it again in a week because the one you spent a day installing has also crapped out.

THE PACK RAT Owner will find all sorts of things, presenting items to the staff like Santa coming down the chimney. These gifts are usually met with raised eyebrow reactions. Salvaged To-Go containers from a restaurant that had suffered a fire is disturbing to say the least. You know the white styrofoam, clamshell To-Go containers, very common and not expensive. Somehow these containers survived the fire but had a fair amount of smoke damage and were not at all suitable for food. *"These are perfectly good"* says the Pack-Rat as he presents them to his staff back at the Dive. As soon as possible, the staff did the right thing and put them in the dumpster where they belonged. The next morning, Pack-Rat retrieved them. Yes, this owner went into the dumpster to re-salvage the containers and was angry with the staff member who tossed them. Fear Not, the staff ended up throwing them away again, they just had to be more stealthy about it. No one said life was going to be easy working at a Dive.

. . .

NOW BEFORE YOU get all upset with Pack-Rat, please consider this. That same owner is responsible for doing the impossible, not with the To-Go containers but with his bar. He built and opened a bar that became a Dive within a very short amount of time. His intention was never to build a Dive, remember you cannot deliberately create a Dive Bar. His intention was to build a small family restaurant. The kind of person he is and how he operates, ended up inadvertently creating a Dive in record time. A truly amazing happenstance indeed. Within the first year of operation the bar became known around town as a Dive even though Pack-Rat was doing what he thought best to run a nice family restaurant. Additionally, there was never a bar at that location before so locals were only making judgements on his business, nothing previous. His natural talent as an owner created a Dive faster than you can throw back a Mystery Shot. Imagine having the natural ability to create such a beautiful mess with the speed and efficiency that normally takes years of neglect, miss-steps and blunderment. Those of us who appreciate Dive Bar culture know that an individual with these God-like talents is extremely rare and should be applauded. Perhaps cast in bronze so that future generations can appreciate and take selfies next to the statue.

THE SURLY BASTARD type owner is surprisingly the best option for some. These are a special type of Dive Bar owner. They are able to keep even the most unruly guest in line. A Surly Bastard owner is a dream come true for some customers simply because they are not allowed into most other bars. Let's say for example you were recently released from the Supermax in Milwaukee, (We'll wait here if you need to look up the Supermax.) You are now on foot, walking with an issued plastic bag of your belongings and you are lucky for two reasons. First you have a few dollars in your pocket and second, you are in Milwaukee, home of inexpensive yet delicious beer. There's a little bar you remember called "Johnny's Back Door". It should be nearby and thankfully Johnny himself is surly enough to accept you in with open arms. Yes sir, maybe even a complimentary can of Schlitz given to you with a, *"Where ya been kid"* knowing full well what the answer is. A place like Johnny's might help acclimate a weary soul or at least provide some mental relief after witnessing some of Johnny's regulars. The potentially unruly need to self medicate just like the rest of us. If they fear the owner, they will moderate their behavior. Being banned from a Dive Bar is never a good thing. Oh sure the banned customer will brag about it like they're a super-rebel but inside they desperately want back in. Slowly dying because unruliness is what Dives express without crossing the line. They feel a horrible separation anxiety from their home, their house of subtle unruliness. The duration of this ban all depends on the crime. Might be a month, might be a year but when the ban is over they come back. Oh they'll be back don't worry.

MOST DIVES HAVE a list of banned customers, some even post the list on the wall. If you're local to the area it is always surprising to read those names. *"Hey I saw Robert Miller's name on the banned list at the bar. Isn't he like the town council committee guy? What the heck did he do?"* The banned thing is an interesting subject because a Dive will most likely let a customer back in after time, while a nicer establishment will not. If you are banned from a nice place it might be for life. Dives are a little more forgiving. Might be because they are the "Last Stop" for some of us. As a Dive Bar regular you have visited many other establishments. You have settled on this little hole in the wall bar. Like it or not, you are a Dive Bar Regular, the staff has come to know you like family, so if you have a bad night and do something to get yourself banned, there's a good chance you will eventually be forgiven and allowed to return at some point. It is not recommended that you test this theory. If you're banned once, you will always be on thin ice. They let you back in, so now you really need to keep it together. Unfortunately you may have permanently angered some employees that will ask the owner to continue your ban during their shifts. For example, *"Ok listen Billy, we will let you back in but NOT on Tuesday and Thursday nights and Saturday day shifts before 5pm."* This is because you really pissed off Mary who works those shifts. She has refused to deal with your sorry ass ever again.

YOU MIGHT BE ASKING what all this has to do with Dive Bar qualification. The scenarios discussed here are all part of Dive Bar culture. Other businesses do not operate with such haphazard, indiscriminate rules or lack thereof. Anecdotal descriptions are necessary in order to paint an accurate picture of the Dives we love. While visiting you might experience similar incidents which help affirm Dive status. Or maybe now you see it operates more like an efficient family restaurant which means not a Dive at all. It could sway your decision one way or another. Additionally some readers might now see the light, go buy Mary some flowers and beg for forgiveness because they miss their Tuesdays and Thursdays at the local.

AN ABSENTEE OWNER is rare but they do exist. This is someone fortunate to have staff they can trust and enough money so they are not as financially vulnerable if a problem happens in their absence. They come and go with ease and seem to be stress free. Lovable characters with endless stories that sound made up until someone corroborates it all and you think, *"Wow, that dude really has experienced some sh*t."* Even if the owner lives out of state most of the time, they can still have a huge impact on their bar. Returning occasionally with stories of grandeur like Teddy Roosevelt coming back from the Amazon jungle. Surrounded by regulars who are ready to call him out, tell him he's full of it. All indirect ways of saying we missed you, come back more often.

TYPICALLY THOUGH, Dive owners work at their bar. They are more hands-on with regular weekly shifts, maybe a lot of them. It's another aspect that makes Dives different from a corporate or chain situation. It's important to mention because there are places without any Dive Bars. People in those places are unaware of the amazing Dive phenomenon. Chain restaurants have a theme while Dive Bars have legitimate character, real and undeniable. People love this Dive character and find it far more interesting than the cookie-cutter predictability found at chains. Sure a chain is a safe option for the family but wouldn't you rather experience some outright foolishness and complete lack of good sense you know the Dive will serve up...

yes...   yes you would my friend.

<u>Hey, what rock did they turn over to find this employee?</u>

IT TAKES a certain type of person to work successfully at a Dive Bar. The average restaurant employs all sorts of people but at a Dive it helps to have experience and thick skin or at least be as crazy as your craziest customer. The average shift at a Dive might seem completely nuts when compared to an ordinary restaurant shift. If you are working at a Dive and are new to the restaurant industry, regulars will pick up on this immediately, *"Poor kid won't last through the day."* Staff at a Dive Bar are some of the most experienced and/or insane, bizarre, tolerant, let's say different from a typical restaurant employee. If not, they either learn fast or quit.

THE TYPE of experience needed is more situational management than how to make a cocktail. Dive bar drinks are usually easy recipes like Jack & Coke or a simple beer so the job becomes more about how you handle the people and their various levels of mental illness. Dive Bar customers can be some of the best and worst in the industry. The average customer just wants to self medicate, needs a drink and is doing this with calm decency. There are others that seem to need a lot of attention so you give it to them, *"Why are you so loud tonight Kevin? Do you need me to call you a cab? Kevin, do you need attention? Sorry every- one, hold on, look at Kevin he needs attention..."* The individual singled out may have actually needed some attention. This also invites others to commence some friendly ridicule. Dive Bar staff develop situational management skills inadvertently through a natural technique of self preservation. Every single shift brings with it nonsense only a Dive can teach. These skills become finely honed. Generally, Dive employees are not shy or afraid to shut people down in any way. They are strong willed enough to calmly handle situations that might get a customer banned for life at a "nicer" establishment. Customers that push the limits know they are wrong or maybe they're just hammered (or both.) This kind of customer is not appreciated by anyone but at a Dive it is less surprising. Dive employees are good at shutting down nonsense because they don't want to get stuck with a bar full of Jackwagons. It's the unfortunate yet constant battle as Dive staff will attest. One thing to keep in mind is owners and staff all know each other from bar to bar, restaurant to restaurant. As soon as a bad incident occurs, names or descriptions spread like wildfire. It's best to stay on the good side of this equation.

DIVE EMPLOYEES MIGHT BE a little on the crazy, different, let's say on the unique side. This can help when dealing with crazy customers because both are speaking the same sort of language. Effective communication is always a good thing. There are many businesses that won't hire anyone outside of the main-stream even though they claim to be equal opportunity. Eclectic or unique individuals might consider Dive Bar employment as something that works for them. We all need to make a living, besides the bank teller job would have started at minimum wage so they might be happier as a Dive employee making a little more scratch and the Dive probably lets her be as expressive as her creativity can reach. The average Human Resources depart-ment might beg to differ with some of this but those in the restaurant industry have a slightly altered version of H.R. regula-tions. When Jane is told by the bank that *"...piercings need to be removed, its company policy."* Jane can respond, *"No problem, I've got a job already. Thank you for the opportunity"*. You see, Jane is polite and is now making more money at Frank's Lounge. Not to mention that Frank's regulars love her style. There's a home for all of us, maybe yours is a Dive?

Staffing at most Dives is usually lean and mean. Your bartender is also your server. That means only one person working the front of the house unless it tends to fill up so another person may be working during the busy period. There will only be one person on duty in the kitchen, if they even have a kitchen. There may only be one person on duty over all. Down and dirty, no kitchen, no server, just one bartender on duty. Have a Slim Jim and like it or you can go two doors down and pick up a pizza if you want. The bartender might have a collection of take-out menus from nearby establishments. Welcome, you have arrived at a Dive Bar.

Customers & Regulars

For the record, a "Regular" is simply a customer who is a frequent visitor to a particular bar. Most bartenders also have their own regular customers. People enjoy going to a place or visiting a person they are familiar with. If they visit often enough they become a "Regular".

THE TYPE of regular customers a bar gets can say a lot about how that bar is perceived generally. The business is open to the public so everyone is welcome but many bars have a particular personality that attracts a certain type of customer. Sports Bars for sports fans, Chain restaurants are safe for families, perhaps the type of music that is hired to perform attracts a certain age group and so on. There are no restrictions like this in a Dive Bar except maybe age. One should be of legal drinking age if booze is all they sell. Parents usually prefer not to expose their children to potentially crazy environments or the foul-mouth dude who is entirely unaware of his mouth anyway. However, back in the day, some parents might stretch this unwritten rule. *"Are you talking about the old Irish Rose, I grew up there! My Dad used to bring me into that place all the time, he'd buy me a bag of peanuts and tell me to keep quiet."* Might explain why little Johnny used colorful language at the holiday dinner table.

. . .

REGULARS at a dive bar are the most loyal in the business, probably loyal to a fault. They spend, on average, more time at their favorite spot than they do in their own home (wasn't supposed to mention that again.) They are also professional drinkers, meaning they like to drink, do it often and are not shy about this. They know what they like and usually want a good amount of it. If a regular doesn't consume their usual amount, a bartender might ask if they're ok. *"You feelin' alright Jimmy? You've only had two beers."* The usual response is something about having to be up early the next morning but it gives the bartender a chance to assess if the customer actually is ok. As much as we should all be self sufficient, it's good to know that others in your Dive family are there for you.

SOME REGULARS ARE SO FREQUENT, they have their own bar stool, might even have their name on that stool. A little brass plate, engraved with a name claiming the stool as theirs. Usually includes a nickname in quotes. Something like *Earl "Buckey" Johnson*. These brass plates are met with varied reactions. Some regulars love them, some do not. Those that don't like them appreciate the staff and owner but would rather keep a lower profile. Perhaps the nameplate becomes an unwanted reminder of how much they drink. Whatever the reason, some even start limiting their time at the bar after a brass plate presentation, while others love it and will bask in the glory, pointing out the name plate and carrying on with blow-hard shenanigans until a friend insists they shut the heck up... please.

REGULARS WILL REMIND a rookie that they are sitting in a coveted seat. *"Hey you know you're in Smitty's seat there and he's about to come in"*. (Now looking at his watch), *"Yup it's three thirty, he's about to come in"*. This means he'd rather sit next to *Leonard "Smitty" Smith* than sit next to you so you'd better just get out of the stool. It's part of playing your cards right, especially if you are not a regular at that bar.

HERE'S what typically happens if you do NOT get off the stool. When Smitty arrives the first guy says, *"Hey Smitty, I told this guy he was in your seat."* Smitty's will say something like, *"That's nice Brian, you still owe me 20 bucks and just let the guy sit there. I don't care."* You see Smitty is actually a good guy so you could give him the seat. At this point the Bartender might intervene, perhaps offering the Yahtzee dice to Brian, *"You still owe him that $20? Why don't you try your luck at the dice Brian".* (Yahtzee dice description is in the Patron Activities section of Maguire's Dive Points List within Chapter 8 and in various other parts of this book)

SADLY, some nameplates are presented posthumously so the bar can continue a legacy of sorts. Regulars make up odd rules as well. For instance, *"If you sit in that seat, you gotta drink Buckey's drink".* Depending on the tenacity of the regulars you may have to actually drink what Buckey used to drink. In reality it's just a way to pay tribute to their friend that passed. Besides, Buckey probably drank something basic like Bud Light so it's best to have one in his memory and listen to a few stories. Obviously he was loved well enough to have an engraved name plate on the stool you happened to sit in.

IF THE STAFF knows you are a complete mess and cannot handle your booze you might still be welcome BUT your drinks will most likely be poured accordingly, (as in weak.) They've learned the hard way about this and merely want to do everyone a favor, including you. Seeing firsthand the long term effects of alcohol is a tough part of the business. It's sort of the elephant in the room that no one talks about. So when Lenny, in his 80's, had several more than his usual *"Couple of pops on the way home"* and it's now snowing outside, someone will give him a ride home. No one wants to hear bad news about him in the morning, especially if they could have done something. Any good establishment will help find a ride for this scenario. However, at a Dive, the ride will also stop for a few groceries, shovel the walkway and help get Lenny and his groceries inside before they return to the bar themselves. The next time you see Lenny he'll have a story about how they offered him a drag off their funny cigarette while they were shoveling his walkway. *"Hey let me tell ya, that cigarette they had there, whoa boy there, wow. I slept like a baby that night"*.

SOME REGULARS GET creative when it comes to paying their bar tabs. Homemade gummy bears for example might be offered to a bartender if the cash is short. Not exactly a bad option even if the bartender does not partake in THC. One can always find a taker for such a product so re-gifting is an option. One story of creativity is more true to the word. An artist in Provincetown, Massachusetts would paint portraits of his fellow regulars. This certainly helped keep the artist's glass full throughout the season.

Original portraits of esteemed regulars hang at the Old Colony Tap

The Old Colony Tap or "O.C." as locals refer to it, is a truly amazing example of Dive Bar culture on every level. A well seasoned bar that's been around for decades and hopefully never changes. Why change perfection after all?

*Harmonica, cigarette lighter and fishing hook clip are
necessary items sometimes*

One regular of the O.C. was describing the numerous jobs he

works, fishing boats and various trades, etc. He was proud of the work he had done to refinish the floor, bar top and tables at the O.C. During the off-season he could easily find affordable rentals to live in but in-season was a completely different story. Rents become so high in the summer that he resorted to sleeping "under the boat." This rustic (to say the least) sixteen foot wooden dory boat, upside down on the sand is not the worst place one could choose for summertime lodging. There were a couple of these boats sitting upside down not far from the water's edge so he had his choice of waterfront living. It's a great example of Can-Do resilience of a Dive Bar Regular. He further explained that he had, *"...dug out the sand all nice so I can sit up."* He even ran an extension cord so he could charge his phone. Hey you're living under a boat, why not poach a little power from the building next door. A concerned listener asked, *"What if the owner of the boat shows up?"* His response, *"These boats? ...these boats haven't moved in years."*

Decades of wear, carefully preserved on this tabletop

Your Dive Bar family may not be apparent at first but if you become a regular, they might love you more than your actual family. Does your family even know you enjoy Metaxa 5 Star and keep a bottle of it hidden under the bar just for you? Many find this sort of community at church. The Dive Bar regular says, *"I am at church."* Besides there's a velvet Jesus hanging over by the jukebox, reminding us all to be kind to each other, that counts. Two unfortunate side effects from drinking are loss of patience, and of course, the long term health effects which some describe as diminishing returns, meaning shortened life. Dive regulars are professional drinkers. They deal with these two side effects all the time. They are not amateurs. The point is, hold it together. Go out and enjoy your favorite bars but not to the point where you become a burden on the people around you. Professionals are always welcome.

Attitude - It's a concept
"I've been to that bar before, it's just not my kind of place"

SOMETIMES PEOPLE HAVE a bad opinion about a bar. *"That place is awful, don't ever go there!"*. Then you discover it's actually a great place and is now one of your favorite stops. Dive's aren't for everyone yet most just need a quick introduction. Be careful you might get hooked. A bar's "Attitude" is basically the temperament of the people inside. If the bar is known as disreputable or worse, this is entirely caused by the owner, staff and regulars. This environment can be caustic to some and inviting to others. It's important to keep in mind because Attitude is the most subjective aspect when considering the Dive Bar subject. Attitude has been deliberately left off of Maguire's Dive Points List because it's just too subjective. There are bars you can visit where the Attitude is so bad that it makes the average Dive seem like Candy Land. You must look for Dive Points beyond Attitude if you want to score Dive Status. Attitude is perceived differently by everyone. Some people thrive in a bad environment while others pass, never to return. It is, however, a great conversation topic.

IMAGINE SITTING at a bar with regulars carrying on about gambling and wild women. The door swings open letting in a blast of sunshine making everyone squint to see who's about to enter. It's a man in his mid thirties but he stops to hold the door and is helping a young woman who is pushing a baby carriage. The presumed father holds the door, lifting the front wheels awkwardly side to side so the carriage can get over the threshold. One of the more outspoken regulars yells from his barstool, *"Whadda ya got in the carriage, a case of Jack Daniels?!?"*. This gets a laugh from everyone in the room except the two at the door with the carriage who now realize they probably can't get lunch at this establishment unless they're looking for peanuts and Blue Ribbon. Don't feel sorry for the young couple, one of the parents should have gone inside first to check things out. Nevertheless the Attitude of the bar was expressed by the regular who yelled the comment. This sort of Attitude can range from a polite suggestion to outright rudeness or worse. Over time an attitude has developed at the bar, sort of an unwritten set of rules and behaviors. No one ever said the baby carriage wasn't welcome but the regulars knew it wasn't a good idea. Most staff in this situation would simply walk over and suggest a different place for lunch and hold the door as the couple retreats back into the light with their carriage. A place where regulars yell obnoxious comments at a young couple should provide plenty of Dive Points beyond the Attitude.

ON THE OTHER hand the young couple might be bringing Junior out to visit Uncle Al who happens to be the guy who yelled the *"...case of Jack Daniels"* comment. The couple might have realized the only way Uncle Al is going to see the new member of the family is to go visit him at his local haunt. This may have been a deliberate move by the couple to blow up their uncle's spot. The others will remind Al that he should be a better uncle from now on.

Another reason Attitude is not calculated for Dive Points is because it's almost impossible to gauge on one or two visits. It's a moving target and better judged when experienced over time. It can change or evolve, a new owner can come in and change things one way or another. Regulars might say, *"Oh ya it was way worse when Bobby owned the place, fights and stuff all the time but the new guy, he's been tryin' to clean it up. It's better now"*. When regulars appreciate this kind of change, it's safe to say the bar's Attitude went too far in the wrong direction. A bar's Attitude might also change when a new bartender comes on or by which regulars are currently drinking. Certain bartenders run things so loosely that their bar becomes a free for all. It may sound like fun but no business can survive by giving away product like a drunken sailor, (just an expression, nothing against the Navy or people who sail and drink.)

ATTITUDE IS THERE for your entertainment, lots of personality along with it. No Dive Points awarded for Attitude but it's still a source of Dive amusement. One important piece of advice on this, is to pay attention to the people who are influencing the bar's attitude. They will probably demonstrate activities that could be worth Dive Points. In particular the "Patron Activities" section of Maguire's Dive Points' List covered in Chapter 8.

5

RESTROOMS

Creativity is boundless

Public Restrooms anywhere can be an experience. Fancy hotels might have a restroom nicer than the living room at your house. On the other hand, some restrooms are completely disgusting, enough to give you a revulsion disorder. We've all experienced restrooms on the nastier side. One might think Dive restrooms would lean towards the disgusting but most of them are completely serviceable. However, Dive restrooms will have something different about them. Such as gentlemen need to walk behind the bar to get to the men's room.

Men's Room door

Bar

Creative floor plan design

Some of the most creative restrooms out there are at Dives so be sure to pay attention while visiting. The Restroom section of Maguire's Dive Points List contains a fair opportunity to pick up some respectable points for your assessment.

The Trough Urinal is a Holy Grail moment.

If you have never seen one they are a real treat. The trough urinal is worth considerable Dive Points. They are disappearing from use and are considered rare. If renovations are made to a men's room, troughs are usually replaced with a conventional urinal. The trough was intended to speed things up and allow several men to go at the same time which by today's standards is considered a little odd, perhaps completely odd.

Trough urinal with plumbing... fancy

Trough not plumbed, would be filled with ice on busy nights

Most men will simply wait and give the current user some privacy. This defeats the original purpose of a trough so replacing them happens often. The novelty of finding a trough is unique enough that a man might mention it upon returning. *"Hey they've got one of those trough things in the men's room."* Odd but true, perhaps the trough conjures up horrifying memories of being a kid at a ball game or other large public event and experiencing one for the first time. Naturally they are only in a men's room so ladies it's up to you if you want to see if one exists. They are a rare novelty worth -20 Dive Points so keep your ears open, you might hear a fellow customer say, *"Oh ya, there's one in the men's room, go take a look"*. Use discretion please.

RESTROOMS AT A DIVE seem like an afterthought. It's as if they built the bar and then someone said, *"Oh geez, what about the toilets?"* Dive restrooms are usually small.

One person at a time, no palatial expanse of luxury but who cares. You might also find unconventional plumbing, self-closing flush handles not originally intended for use with restroom fixtures or storage for empty beer bottles next to the toilet or a microwave oven or in this case both, (see picture, huge Dive Points there.)

Perfectly serviceable and includes a creative drain pipe

"Springback" flush handle with antiqued patina finish

Storage for empty beer bottles and a convenient
microwave oven

Some restrooms are just awkwardly designed. For example, there's not enough room to open the stall door if someone is standing at the urinal. These small confines can create logistical nightmares but it's all part of the charm at Dives. Cracked porcelain repaired with construction adhesive is another Dive favorite.

This usually happens because a frustrated customer has somehow smashed the toilet bowl, sink or other porcelain fixture.

Lovely

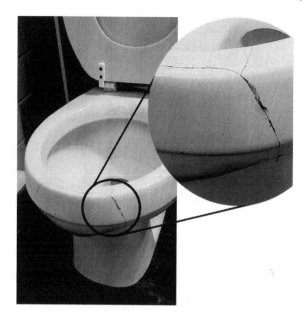

The repair is to simply glue it back together with heavy duty construction adhesive. Not a pretty fix but it usually does the trick. You may have seen this and thought, *"What happened here, this toilet is all cracked?"* Well, now you know and now you can make a mental note of these points for your assessment. The ingenuity and "Can-Do" attitude it takes to glue a toilet back together should be rewarded with Dive Points, so don't forget.

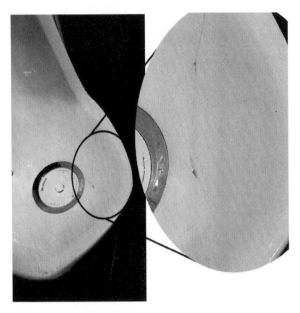

Nice repair job, barely noticeable = less divey

THE CHARM of Dive restrooms can be humorous and might include a "Singularity" (definition discussed in the next chapter.) If there is carpeting right up and around the toilets, that might be disgusting in the eyes of some but it's worth Dive Points. The "Death Step" as it was called by regulars of one bar, was extremely charming. Upon entering the mens room if you happened to step too far to the right you could fall into the basement and snap your neck. Somehow, inebriated customers would simply walk past this without issue. Eventually the floor was repaired but that hazard was around long enough for regulars to name it. Thankfully no one was injured in the year (or more) of its existence.

. . .

NEW ORLEANS' own, Snake and Jake's provides us with this wonderful example of restroom beautification.

You can see the walls have been adorned by some local artists who thoughtfully brought their own set of art supplies. It is far from the most disgusting of restrooms. When you first looked at this photo you may have thought there were a ton of Dive Points but an accurate tally yields -20 from this restroom. The cleverly adorned graffiti walls provide -10 Dive Points, Small "One at a time" size is -5 and there was some awkwardness regarding the hallway and floor so another -5. It's important to be objective and fair when accounting for Dive Points. Chapter 8 contains the complete list of all Dive Points so don't worry about the specifics of that just yet.

6

THE SINGULARITY

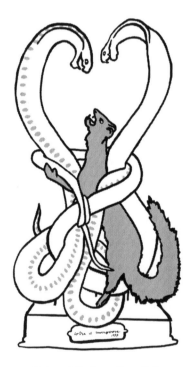

Outward displays of creativity

Have you ever been in a bar and seen a piece of decor that makes you think, *"well that's weird"*. You might have been looking at a Singularity. The Oxford English Dictionary defines the word Singularity as *The state, fact, quality, or condition of being singular.* For our purposes, pertaining to Dive Bars the definition shall be: *A structural attribute or item displayed at a bar (inside or out) or something about a bar that is unique and also adds to the bar's divey atmosphere.* Henceforth known as a Singularity. They are extremely important to note because they add a lot of personality to the bar in a beautiful way that not only says you're at a Dive, it also speaks about the owner's creativity. Singularities often reflect much about the owner and their flair for barroom decor or maybe a creative idea of how to renovate the building. Could also be a unique theme, maybe humorous in a #onlyataDiveBar kind of way. Dive owners are unique people with distinctly advanced taste. This usually means over time they have added to their bars in ways that express character and uniqueness.

Singularities could be a kitschy piece of decor such as something found at a flea market, *"Oh this would be great for the bar"* as they purchase with glee.

Beloved mascot "Woodcock" at Bob O'Malley's
Whaleback Restaurant, Cape Cod

It might be something you first think is completely normal like a bumper pool table but after further consideration you realize bumper pool was created for small spaces like in people's basement game rooms. This particular table is coin operated and more heavy duty, stout construction. Clearly it was built for a bar room, making it far less common.

Vintage, coin operated Bumper Pool table

They might be elusive at first but when you discover one it will stand out in a way that says *This is a Singularity*. It is unique to this bar only or at least not at all common. Examples are provided here in order to help you recognize them and become a Singularity expert.

THIS FIELD of staples and hooks is in the graffitied ceiling of a bar, left behind after years of multiple events and hanging streamers and decorations.

Graffitied ceiling with staples

Not decor itself but considered a Singularity because it displays a certain type of attitude consistent with Dive Bar mentality. No time to remove the old stapes because the next event is upon us. The new round of streamers and banners need to be hung immediately. Plus we can use the existing staples already in place to hang the new round of decorations, genius. Nevertheless, Singularities should be one of a kind or at least uncommon, possibly humorous, distinctive, down right stupid or all the above. A genuine Dive will have at least one Singularity. When you discover one it will bring a smile to your face and a sense of awe in your Dive Appreciateur heart. They are worth a lot on Maguire's Dive Points List so keep your eyes out for them.

SINGULARITIES HELP COMMUNICATE you are definitely at a Dive Bar. The microwave in the restroom is one for sure or a simple message written on human bones, both lovely examples.

Human bones with a written warning

The average customer might think nothing about them but a Dive Professional knows it's completely insane, a joy to behold, a Dive Wonderment. They are very important and help us appreciate our favorite bars but be sure not to award Singularity points for something that doesn't deserve it. Determination might be difficult because of the subjective nature so it's helpful to get a second opinion. If you are questioning whether something is a Singularity, here are some points to consider.

1. Is the item unique or at least rare?

2. Is the item humorous in some way?

3. ARE THERE ELEMENTS OF "WTF" about this?

. . .

4. Is there a story behind the item such as how it was acquired, (There's always a story)

5. Can any other bar claim this Theme or Uniqueness

IF YOU ANSWERED *yes* to most of those then you probably have a Singularity. Some bars have a theme.

FOR EXAMPLE the Flamingo Sports Bar in St. Petersburg, Florida has claim to a Jack Kerouac kind of theme.

Jack Kerouac mural at the Flamingo Sports Bar, St.
Petersburg, FL. Photo courtesy of Mike James

Mr. Kerouac had frequented this bar before he passed away.
The bar has carried on a tradition of sorts and it's fair to say that
no other bar would be able to claim this. Therefore a Singularity
exists by way of a unique theme. It is not a physical piece of
decor but still considered a Singularity because it's uniqueness.
Also Jack Kerouac was known to imbibe, play pool, smoke ciga-
rettes etc. His persona fits well with this bar. He wasn't just a
celebrity who stopped in for a photo opportunity. He had been a
part of the bar's family so to speak. Therefore Singularity points
should be awarded.

. . .

A LOVELY PIECE of decorum like the "Never Ending Toilet Paper Roll", (perhaps the only one in existence) was in the men's room at Bob O'Malley's Whaleback Restaurant on Cape Cod, Massachusetts.

"Never Ending" toilet paper roll

Before renovations, the men's room was wonderfully equipped with this immense roll of toilet paper. It can be deemed a Singularity because of it's humorous nature and uniqueness. Singularities can also be a great conversation piece and might even get stolen, then magically return somehow. Unfortunately, the big paper roll at the Whaleback was removed during renovations and is still in storage (at the time of publication.) This is Not Good, the bar lost Dive Points because of these changes. First, the men's room should not have been renovated. It was perfectly lovely as is. Secondly the unique paper roll should have been reinstalled, not replaced with a new contemporary dispenser. The roll was *"...put in the basement"*, which is completely unacceptable. A petition is underway to have the "Never Ending Toilet Paper Roll" returned to its rightful location within the men's room. Thank you.

RESTAURANTS AND BARS that are not Dives simply will not have Singularities. Owners and managers of Non-Dives typically want to project a more mainstream image so the Singularity never gets installed. It's also possible the owner's spouse or friends will offer opinions that nix having a Singularity at their establishment. *"Seriously George, I love you but that taxidermy collection is disgusting and turns people off. You've got to get rid of it."*

An entertaining ceiling display of taxidermy and whatnot

Dives are more casual, they welcome things that make the bar stand out. Especially if it means standing out in a uniquely peculiar way.

A SINGULARITY MIGHT ALSO BE a person. An individual closely associated with the bar like an owner, staff or regular. For a person to be a Singularity they must truly be unique.

"WHAT'S THIS YOU SAY? We must meet this amazing individual at once."

AS YOU MIGHT IMAGINE, someone who qualifies for this title would be held in high regard. The Stone Rooster in Marion, Massachusetts, was owned and operated by a woman who fit this description. Her name is Gilda, she has since retired from the bar business but her bar was a stand alone building that more resembles a roadhouse you might find in southern states.

Gilda's Stone Rooster, Marion, MA

Part of the decor inside is Gilda's wall of photographs. It speaks of her appreciation for numerous friends throughout the decades. Before she retired at the age of 97, it was safe to say that Gilda was the most experienced bartender around. Gilda lived upstairs and ran the bar on the ground floor. She had an active calendar of live music in particular Big Band and Jazz. making her bar one of the few Jazz clubs in the area. A person in their late 90s who is still actively running a business and working shifts is pretty incredible on it's own.

Gilda (on right) watches the South Coast Brass Band
perform at the Stone Rooster in 2018

Gilda is one of the most interesting people you could meet and she puts up with nothing. Those who don't understand this are brought up to speed quickly by Gilda's sharp, witty retort. A man and woman seated at her bar asked for their check. Gilda told them it's $11.50; you only had the two drinks. The man said, *"I've got this"* as he held out a credit card. Gilda looked at him and said, *"Sorry we're cash only here"* as she pointed to the signs stating this. *"Cash Only?!?"* the man replied as he began to defend himself and cause a scene, *"Who's cash only anymore, who doesn't take credit, come on now..."*. Gilda just stared at him in deadpan silence until he was finished ranting. Then Gilda slowly turned to the woman and said, *"Honey, you are SO lucky."*

DURING GILDA'S tenure at the Stone Rooster she had become very well known in the area. Her individual nature and uniqueness always stole the show. Those who have met her would agree. She's a one of a kind character who had been slinging drinks longer than most of her customers had been alive. She herself probably would not have considered her bar a Dive even though many others did. It's always important to consider other viewpoints when discussing this Dive Bar subject. Not everyone thinks that being a Dive is a wonderful accomplishment, (though they should.)

SO A SINGULARITY CAN BE many things from a unique object, artwork, a rare item or theme to an owner or person who stands out in any crowd to a bizarre renovation or something about the building that speaks to the owner's unconventional thought process. Every good Dive has something in it or about it that makes it unique. Singularities are the notable way to accomplish this so they carry a large Dive Point value. Be sure you appreciate every Singularity you come across and award Dive Points appropriately.

7

DID COVID KILL THE DIVE BAR?

A tragedy befallen the unexpected

THE ENTIRE PLANET BECAME EXHAUSTED WITH IT. THE COVID-19 pandemic is a subject which conjures up mixed feelings for everyone. The mandates issued by our government leaders affected everyone and Dive Bars for sure. Real Dives closed their doors at the start of lockdown and may have NEVER reopened. It's extremely important to note this because of the sheer impact on Dive Bars in particular. The virus subject should be taken seriously. A variety of opinions exists on the protocol and what we all should have done to get through safely. That said, the mandates and regulations that many businesses had to comply with in order to remain open caused some scenarios worth discussing. The incidents presented here are not intended to make light of the pandemic but are real and factual nonetheless.

FOR THE SAKE OF CLARIFICATION, on or about March 17th 2020, Governors across the United States issued mandates requiring most businesses to close their doors in an effort to control the spread of the Covid-19 virus. A short list of businesses were allowed to remain open having been declared "Essential". Bars and Restaurants were NOT considered essential and remained shuttered initially until restrictions eased up. However, Dive Bars, that is REAL Dives, remained closed because they did not serve food, thus considered not essential. At first many Dives tried to re-open. Pointing out they offer food like Peanuts and Pretzels (hopefully Slim Jims too.) Some bars simply charged each customer for a bag of snack food like potato chips. Inexpensive so you didn't care, you just got your drink, felt more normal and were in compliance because you had purchased "food". Many considered the Bag of Chips as the saving grace for Dive Bars without kitchens. The Covid restrictions were a hassle but hey all Dives needed to do is offer some snacks to remain open. Officials then further tightened restrictions, making the mandate more specific. Hot, prepared in-house types of foods were required forcing many Dives to close again or figure out a menu that worked.

.   .   .

NOW THE FUN STARTS. The state mandates offered an amazingly ridiculous gray area for bar and restaurant owners to operate in. Owners would educate themselves (or not) to the particulars and then make decisions on how they were going to run their business. It was a Brave New World out there. The average restaurant serves hot, in-house prepared food so they only concern themselves with other sections of the mandate like distancing, offering hand sanitizer, etc, the list goes on. However, if a Dive owner wanted to stay open they had to comply with all of that AND create a food menu acceptable to... well... an authority that might show up and check on them if they didn't offer the proper hot food. That compliance was left up to individual cities and towns to enforce. Which further amplified the gray area interpretations. A wonderful scenario to attempt making a profit in. Enforcement of these "rules" fell mainly on local Health Departments. Local police were smart to point out these matters are not within their purview. Health inspectors everywhere were now expected to keep an eye on the huge array of compliance and safety issues added to their already busy workload, not a position of envy. Some communities went as far as hiring additional staff in order to help cover these new responsibilities. The new employees, officially named Covid Ambassadors, were immediately called "Covid Police" by everyone else and away we go.

HAVING to deal with an ever changing set of rules was such a hassle that many Dives chose to remain closed. If an owner chose to stay open during all this mess they needed to come up with some food offerings simple enough so that Bill, who's been working on Tuesday and Thursday nights since the beginning of time itself, can handle this new food thing. Hey, remember the kitchen? As a Real Dive, you might have a kitchen of some sort but you have not used it as a kitchen in years. You need to clean out your office and turn it back into a kitchen, oh the joy. You've already reassured Billy that it's not going to be anything crazy, some Hot Dogs maybe. Thankfully you also have Maryellen on staff who says she'll make meatballs and your new menu is complete. Hotdogs from the steamer that Billy remembered, now dragged from storage and cleaned up, along with a crock-pot of meatballs and sauce when Maryellen isn't tired of making them. Down home basic goodness that everyone loves.

BILLY'S REGULARS from back in the day remember the old hotdog steamer. *"You still have that thing? Good Lawd."* They might even add, *"You should never have cleaned it, the patina inside makes 'em taste better."* Some of the pandemic menus created by Dives would vary daily depending on how the staff was feeling. *"Do you really want me to set up the hotdog steamer??? How about I get some pizza delivered, so you guys can shut up."* Oddly many customers started looking forward to a hotdog from their favorite Haunt. At first, staff might consider leaving the used paper plates, napkins, etc. on the tables. That way if an inspector happens to stop by it looks more obvious that food is being sold along with the usual beverages. The menu might be so inexpensive that a customer would say, *"Just charge me for a hotdog so it's on the tab, I already ate. I'm just drinking now."* A printed record of the food purchase being enough to remain compliant with the mandates.

THEN A NATURALLY BEAUTIFUL PROGRESSION HAPPENED. We all knew it was just a matter of time. If there's one thing that Dives are good at, it's finding Loopholes. The Real Dive, the one you love, the one with no kitchen, the one that jumped through hoops trying to stay open, had a realization. They looked in the mirror and said, "We are cash only" then they repeated it louder with excitement, "WE ARE CASH ONLY." They burst onto the streets singing in joyous harmony, "WE'RE - CASH - ONLY, WE'RE - CASH - ONLY." This realization was huge. Cash only means there are no printed checks, no specific record of purchases one way or another. If an inspector showed up, they had no choice but to take your word for it. *"Yes sir, all the customers here have enjoyed their lunch food, yes sir, isn't that right Sammy?"* Let's face it, customers want to be compliant just like the house does. Everyone was immediately on board with this new unwritten, never discussed Covid Food purchase policy. It goes perfectly with the "Look the Other Way" rebel attitude that Dives project solidly. Besides Billy has been setting up the hotdog steamer for old time sake and good faith covid effort that helped the bar seem pretty much in compliance. No doubt there were inspectors that shook their heads and walked away. In fact that's exactly what happened. No one officially announced the start or end of spot check inspections but it's safe to assume the authorities pulled the plug on that program early on. Inspections seemed to dissipate and go away all together.

THERE WERE some extremely unfortunate inspections that should be considered unfair. Demands put on restaurants that were already under extreme regulations caused owners to jump through even more hoops or just close up shop, all in the name of power trip inspectors. The restaurant and bar industry was hit hard with regulations and protocol that varied widely from state to state. These inconsistencies caused confusion, frustration and a Go "F" Yourself attitude from many in the service industry. One place gets away with murder while another place is forced to completely revamp their menu. This was unfair, inconsistent and frankly stupid. It became a battle between civil liberties and public safety with restaurants stuck in the middle. Thankfully the frequency of inspections died off. A wise decision because everyone's stress levels were at the breaking point.

IF THE REPORTED number of Covid-19 cases increased the restrictions would tighten. It was a weekly back and forth battle with numbers and protocol. Florida might be the exception and other states perhaps. This is not a criticism of any region, just a simple observation. Central Florida is a wonderful hunting ground for Dives Bars. The state mandates there were different enough and most likely kept Dives from having to close.

SADLY THERE WERE many Dives that chose not to open at all during the pandemic. Covid protocols were considered too much of a hassle. The longer the restrictions dragged on some eventually decided to reopen. Install some plexiglass dividers and give it a shot. Those of us who love Dives were overjoyed with these reopenings, comparing it to visiting a long lost friend after a natural disaster had forced a separation.

IF ALL THAT wasn't enough, being closed gave owners and staff time to make improvements. Here you have a perfectly good Dive Bar and now that you're closed you've got a chance to clean up, paint, make improvements etc. ALL of which changes your Dive score, most definitely in the wrong direction, as in less of a Dive. Lets say your Dive score was a solid 165, a pandemic shows up and gives a chance to clean up around the place. Sounds great, BUT not if you're trying to maintain that Dive level. No Sir, improvements of any kind will almost always make you less of a Dive. This unfortunate situation was more common than you might imagine. Years of neglect washed away in seconds by an owner and staff who were merely trying to keep busy during lockdown. A tragedy befallen the unexpected. Remember if the staff cleans things up, paints the restrooms, fixes the hole that Phillip punched in the wall, they are changing their Dive Status in the wrong direction. Tell them to knock it off, you prefer things left as is. Hopefully your favorite Dive never closed and is still thriving out there in it's beautifully abysmal pre-pandemic state.

8

MAGUIRE'S DIVE BAR QUALIFICATION SYSTEM AND HOW
TO USE IT

IMAGINE HAVING AN EARLY LUNCH DOWN BY THE TRACKS ON A
beautiful summer day. Your meal includes a Pickled Egg, Slim
Jims and a glass of Wild Irish Rose, while you play your lottery
numbers and consider ordering a Mystery Shot in the dimly lit
ambiance of your windowless neighborhood haunt. Nothing

better right? If you said yes, then you are a Dive Bar Apprecia-teur. Equally important is that you realize the sheer abundance of Dive Points mentioned there. Bars that offer those wonderful items and provide a particular atmosphere to enjoy them in, should be given credit. These credits are henceforth known as **Dive Points**. Bars work hard to earn these points. As patrons we need to respect and appreciate this. Dive Bars earn these points every day they are open. Conveniently provided here is a comprehensive list of these Dive Points with a brief description and a point value. The list is called **Maguire's Dive Points List**. It will become an invaluable tool for your assessments should you choose to make them. Most importantly, the list helps us realize the numerous and wonderful attributes we may have previously taken for granted. The nuances that were right there under our nose that we now have a better appreciation for. Maguire's Dive Points List has shown us the light.

AFTER GOING through the list and adding up all the Dive Points a bar has earned, you then compare the total on **Maguire's Dive Chart**. This chart displays a range of status that the bar falls into. The list, together with the chart, guides us more accurately on how divey a bar is or not. Maybe the bar you love does not make the cut. That's ok, you can still love it and not being a Dive might be something the owner appreciates. More impor-tantly, is that YOU now see the difference. You were under the impression that your favorite bar was a Dive but the assessment did not qualify that bar as such. Do not take this personally. Everyone should consider all the divey aspects and thus gain an improved appreciation for Dives. On the other hand, if your favorite bar happens to score nice and low then you can rest assured you have experienced the real deal. Appreciation of a great Dive Bar should never be underestimated. Additionally, if your favorite bar does not score as a Dive, it is recommended that you commence a search for one that does. The favorite bar can remain on your list of possible stops but there are other places that need your attention. You are reading this book after all.

Just a few Dive Ethics to mention first...

IF YOU CHOOSE to complete an assessment please do not be *That Guy*. It is important that you get to know the material well enough that you are NOT inside the bar with this book, actively making an assessment. You don't want to look foolish nor do you want to come across rude to the staff. Your task with all this is simple, while at the bar enjoy the Dive Wonderment. Make only mental notes and thus avoid getting tossed out because the bartender thought you were some kind of weird Narc. First and foremost you are there to enjoy a beverage and hopefully some divey offerings. Wait until you have left the bar before you start making any notes. You might discreetly use your cell phone to jot down a brief reminder but never make a complete assessment while inside the bar. The better you know the material on Maguire's Dive Points List, the better you will be at recognizing all the wonderment for an accurate score. Following this guidance should also give you an overall improved appreciation of Dive Bar culture. You were taking part in the live aspects and not writing things or on your phone the whole time. It's similar to taking a video with your cell phone while your favorite band is live on stage. Please, for the love of Pete, put your phone away and enjoy the show.

. . .

IMPORTANT SIDE NOTE: Do Not enter a bar with a large group of people, ever. (Read that sentence over and over until you fully grasp the meaning.) You must believe this in your heart and understand its importance in your life as a person who appreciates a great Dive or just a night out generally. The idea is to be safe but not intrusive. Imagine if you visit a quiet bird sanctuary with a bus load of 3rd Graders jacked up on sugary, caffeinated beverages. Your goal to see birds will be fruitless to say the least. Nothing against 3rd Graders, they are probably more welcome than a group of adults at most places. Regardless, do not entertain this nonsense. A large group would destroy the natural Dive ambiance you are seeking. If you enter alone, order a beverage and merely observe, you will most likely receive what you came for. The "vibe" if you will, must not be disrupted if you want to truly witness the pageantry. Use street smarts and be safe but leave the bus parked at home.

IF YOU'RE a regular at a bar, you've been there many times. You've been able to witness all sorts of amazing Dive Points. You could easily tally up an accurate Dive Point Total in a few minutes just from memory. However, if it's your first visit and you only have a short amount of time at a bar this is where it becomes especially helpful to know the material well. Knowledge of the list also makes you more discreet. Remember you are there to enjoy a beverage and hopefully some divey atmosphere. That ambience is easily disrupted, just say hello to the bartender, order a drink and relax. When you entered, you might have inadvertently disrupted things. Ideally you want the atmosphere to return to normal. As soon as you get a drink that should happen.

. . .

YOU MIGHT BE DRAWN into conversation. If the Regulars don't know you, they might be curious and ask who the heck you are. This is usually a great thing and might help get the natural environment to return. These conversations will most likely be rich with local color and could tell you a lot about the bar. Even if the conversation ends up being completely ridiculous, it's entertaining, and usually a good indication of the type of regular customer there. At the same time you can discreetly look around for divey aspects such as No Menu available but hey, they sell Slim Jims (perfect). You have not set up your laptop and you are not actively taking notes because you know that activity would be disruptive and weird to the degree that you might get your ass kicked. Just rely on observation and memory, let's try to blend in here okay. If you don't understand this it's best not to worry about doing an assessment in the first place.

ANECDOTES, stories and specific examples are provided throughout the book in order to help demonstrate the types of things you're looking for. Some of the most interesting Dive attributes might be harder to spot. Some of these attributes might be unique to that one bar making them very valuable in your assessment. Remember, it's more than just a Dive Point total, one has not fully lived until one has been enriched by the offerings of an authentic Dive Bar.

THE UNIQUE DETAILS that provide rich character make Dives the special places we love. These details vary widely and might include quaint redneck wind chimes.

Creative wind cimes

It is said there is nothing more soothing than the clanking of empty aluminum bottles in a summer breeze. Could also be a conversation with a surly bartender who sets the mood so low that the patrons leave in a state of depression.

Handy Library and ATM

HOW ABOUT A HANDY library service next to the ATM. We will need some cash, they are Cash Only after all. There may also be considerations that you originally took for granted but after reading this book you now realized their divey importance. Ideally one needs to visit a few times in order to make a true and complete assessment. Subsequent visits usually provide new experiences like a dude running outside to puke or perhaps you just noticed the velvet Jesus hanging in the back. Your first visit is usually the most important but if you can, visit often enough to witness and enjoy as much Dive wonderment as possible.

97

Remember you represent yourself and maybe your hometown so make a good impression on the tip jar. If for some reason you don't like tipping or you feel that tips are just wrong for any reason, there is a solution. Simply do not patronize establishments where tipping is expected. If you feel strongly about not tipping it is suggested you hand this book to anyone else then go about your life. No further reading is necessary.

"She works hard for money"

Photo Exercise: Take a look at the next photo. It seems pretty normal, a couple of drinks on the bar with a relatively empty bowl of popcorn, right? After you familiarize yourself with Maguire's Dive Points List you will see there are potentially -40 Dive Points in this seemingly innocent little picture.

The answer key for this exercise is immediately following Maguire's Dive Points List.

THE LIST WAS WRITTEN to be as comprehensive as possible yet short enough not to bore the piss out of the average reader. The main point is to solidly identify Dive Bars and eliminate the gray area doubt and Jackwagonery in the process. You will recognize some aspects immediately and hopefully experience all of them eventually. It is impossible to list every divey aspect. This means you might come across new discoveries of Dive Wonderment. Be sure to appreciate them and if you feel strongly enough, submit them at (www.DiveBarBook.com).

CAN'T SAY THIS ENOUGH,

Please Do Not make your assessment while inside the bar. Just be a customer, have fun, tip well and keep your eyes open for Dive Points. Familiarize yourself with this material so when you are in the bar you can easily recognize Dive Points but most importantly enjoy the bar and hopefully it's amazing Dive atmosphere. Dives are fun but you cannot fully experience them if you are the creepy weird guy sitting at the end of the bar writing things down and taking pictures with your phone. Thank you in advance for your respect.

Be On The Look-Out

Consider the Dive Points List in two ways. First, specific points to account for. Secondly, an overall concept of the things to watch for. This will steer you to notice unique things not on the list but should still be considered. New, unusual, maybe humorous points to make note of. Let's say you score a bar at -110, pretty divey. You also add a side note that might read *"They have these creeky bar stools that are really loud every time someone gets up or down. Every bar stool was loud. It was funny how much noise it made and the bartender said he was planning to oil them soon."* It's important to document these little gems if possible. They give the bar additional character and become an important part of how people might appreciate this Dive.

. . .

MIGHT ALSO BE THIS: *"This Bar is a +60, The place isn't divey at all. Jackwagon friend wasted my good time, don't waste yours, unless you're hungry. They have a great menu."* A little rough maybe but hey, that individual had been steered the wrong way.

IF YOU'VE NEVER DONE this before, take a minute to assess a bar right now. Grab a pen and paper, think of a bar you know well. Can be any bar, Dive or not. This exercise will help you understand the process. Most Dive Point values are negative numbers, be sure to notice that some aspects are positive (+) values in **Bold**. Negative numbers mean Dive, while positive numbers do not.

MAGUIRE'S DIVE POINTS LIST
Achieve Lower Heights

HOURS OF OPERATION - (verify online if needed)
- (-15) Open 24 hours
- (-10) Open by 8am
- (-5) Opens between 8am and 10am
- **+5 (plus 5 points)** Opens after 10am, Operates during Lunch and Dinner Hours only = positive points
- (-5) Opens at 4pm or later (varies), Bar Hours for evening drinking, usually open late afternoon/early evening, stays open till the wee hours. Hours might be 4pm to 3am daily, for example.

• (-10) Random hours, open whenever the helps shows up kind of thing

BASE THE HOURS ON A MAJORITY, If the bar is open 6 days at 8am but closed one day a week that is a majority open at 8am bar.

• ADDITIONAL (-5) Open by 11am on Major Holidays. You may have to ask the staff if the bar opens on Christmas Day for example. If the answer is something like, *"Oh ya, I usually take that shift. Bright and early Christmas Morning"*. Apply the Major Holiday Dive Points in this case.

LOCATION & Exterior

• (-5) "Element of Fear" People who approach the bar for the first time are asking if this is a good idea. Maybe even you are questioning the decision to enter.

• (-5) "LOW RENT DISTRICT" The Bar is in an undesirable location of some sort. Perhaps there is a junk yard next door, etc. (This doesn't mean the owner pays low rent)

• (-5) "THE CLOSED LOOK" Bar looks closed during business hours.

• (-5) BAR'S main entrance is not the front of the building. Front of the building has a door that is always locked or is at least not the popular accepted entrance for this bar.

• (-5) <u>Beer Distributor Sign</u> such as the Budweiser "Bowtie," exterior signage only. You can also award points if the brand is other than Budweiser. These signs are typically installed by the beer company or distributor, the name of the bar is usually smaller text at the bottom. A good Dive will have displayed one for decades.

• (-5) "Unexpected Location" Any place where one would not normally expect to find a bar but it is there anyway. (Snake & Jake's) Snake & Jake's Christmas Club Lounge in New Orleans, nestled between half million dollar homes for example.

• (-5) "Frowning Neighbor" Organization next door or across the street which generally frowns on the consumption of alcohol. Example: The bar is located across from a Rehabilitation Facility, (Churches or Religious buildings also count)

• <u>Additional</u> (-15) "Message of Hope" from the Frowning Neighbor. If a sign is visible from any bar stool or seat inside. The sign might say something about a Rehabilitation, Alcohol Addiction program or a religious message of Hope for those addicted to drugs and alcohol. If you can see that message from any seat in the bar, it's (-15) Dive Points. Take (-5) if the sign only visible from outside the bar.

• (-5) VACANT NEIGHBORS, (empty storefront next to or across the street from the bar)

• (-5) SUPPORT BUSINESS within reasonable walking distance. Customers from the bar will patronize the "Support Business" for necessary items not available from the bar itself. Use your best judgment, convenience store, sandwich shop, pizza, two doors down, something like that.

*Evidence of "Pre-game Activities" with signage reminding people this
activity is no bueno*

• (-5) "PRE-GAME EVIDENCE" near the entrance or in the parking
lot. Bottle caps, nips (airline bottles), empties of any kind not
originating from the bar, indicates customers are drinking outside
beverages in addition to drinking at the bar.

   • Additional (-5) Posted signage advising against this Pre-
game activity.

   • Additional (-15) for BOTH the evidence and the signage. A
well deserved total of -25 Dive Points awarded for blatant disregard of local laws and practices.

• +15 (PLUS **15 points**) Nice views from inside, Ocean, Beach,
Lakefront, Harbor, etc. Don't want to hear about it. A Dive on
the beach is way less dive than a bar without windows, plain and
simple, = **+15**

• • •

• **+15** (PLUS **15 points**) Valet service offered at the door.

• **+5** (PLUS **5 points**) Flowers and/or Plantings outside, if it's just a pot of flowers at the door then ignore this. Apply points only for in the ground, more permanent plantings and also window boxes. Window boxes require a lot of attention which demonstrates non-divey behavior.

INTERIOR AMENITIES **& Decor**

• (-5) Barroom Decor has appreciable dust. This needs to be noticeable dust, as if someone put up the decor and has not touched it in years kind of dust.

• (-5) "CASH ONLY" Bar does not accept credit/debit cards. Cash only transactions

Examples of cash register drawers left open, also note the "Cash Only" sign in the middle picture

• (-10) "Cash Drawer Open" The drawer on the cash register is always open. Do NOT ask why.

"This is why we can't have nice things"

• (-5) Paper signage, Temporary paper signs, made in house, informing customers on a variety of subjects. Not to be confused with event flyers or band posters. These signs are things like "House Rules" or suggestions on behavior that should be obvious but a sign is needed anyhow.

Sticker collection on premises

• (-5) "Sticker Collection" Bar has a beer fridge or cooler with various stickers displayed. Usually a collection of stickers with a wide variety of messages, slogans, jokes, you name it. The fridge glass door might be covered to the degree that one cannot see product inside. Also counts if sticker collection is displayed on something other than a fridge.

• (-5) OWNER LIVES ON THE PREMISES. Owner lives upstairs or "out back in a trailer," etc.

• (-5) PETS INSIDE THE BAR. Only award these points if it goes against the local regulations. If local authorities allow pets inside bars then skip this.

• (-5) WORKING PAY PHONE. Bar maintains a working, coin operated, pay phone.

(-5) Additional if this pay phone is the house phone (i.e. vendors and such call this pay phone as the accepted line for the bar)

(-5) Additional if regulars answer incoming calls on this pay phone. For example, *"Hello Johnny's Pub, how can I help you?" answered by a non-staff member*

• (-5) DISPLAYED photo of past owner(s), R.I.P.

*Only two windows and the majority of both are covered
and blocked with neon signs*

• (-10) No windows (none at all)

Apply (-5) If there are only a few windows covered or blocked somehow. For example there are two windows and both have large neon signs blocking them to the degree that the window is basically ineffective.

• +5 (PLUS **5 points**) Staff wears a uniform or house established clothing

Additional **+5 (plus 5 points)** if necktie is part of the house uniform at any season

(Add these points even if the staff does not wear a necktie in the summer months)

• (-5) STAFF WEARS THEIR OWN CLOTHING, No house uniform required. Staff might wear a logo t-shirt on their own but the house does not have a set uniform.

. . .

• (-5) Bartender totals your check by the amount of time you have been there, not by how many drinks you've had. Example, *"Let's see, there's two of you, been here for a little over an hour, that's $20"*

• (-5) Holiday decorations are still up, out of season. At least one month beyond the date celebrated. Only counts if the theme of the bar is not associated with a particular holiday. For Example, Snake & Jake's Christmas Club Lounge has some Christmas decor all the time. In this case do not apply Dive points. (Fear not Snake & Jake's has plenty of other ways they achieve points)

Basic cement floor

• (-5) Cement Floor, plain old, poured cement floor, not dressed up in any way.

. . .

• (-5) FLOOR TILES BROKEN, missing, cracked and/or neglected

Don't trip, the bartender might not serve you

• (-5) "Stumble Hazard" Weathered floor is uneven or presents a stumble hazard in some way, (can be any type of floor material)

• (-5) CARPETING, especially near the Bar
Additional (-5): Carpet smells bad, sour aroma permeates the room.
Additional (-10): If carpeting is inside the restroom

• (-5) CIGARETTE SMOKE AROMA. These points are only available in places where smoking tobacco is NOT allowed inside bars. The local ordinance does not allow smoking inside yet there are still remnants of this activity inside.

. . .

• (-10) Customers are actively smoking. These points are only available in places where smoking is not allowed inside bars. The local ordinance does not allow smoking of tobacco inside yet customers are doing this anyhow.

• (-5) "Rocks Glass Ashtray" Bar glass is being used for an ashtray.

Rocks Glass used as ashtray

• (-5) "Smokers Paradise" If smoking is allowed legally inside the bar and the majority of patrons take part in this, then award these points. Also award these points if the bar is known as a Smokers Paradise.

• (-5) Eclectic Decor, should generally include things that you would not have or want for yourself. Might be aging and dusty taxidermy, vintage boat parts, velvet artwork (other than Elvis or Jesus such as a velvet tiger), car parts, vintage signs and so on. This does not include Singularities. This is for decor that is more common but still should be noted.

• (-10) Velvet Elvis *or* Velvet Jesus hung proudly on display for public viewing

Jesus and Elvis Presley together, velvet artwork

• (-25) Both Elvis and Jesus together velvet artwork

• (-5) "SUGGESTIVE ARTWORK" Nudes of any kind or suggestive pictures, paintings, posters. These must be on display for the public, anywhere on the premises in order to apply Dive Points.

Beautiful suggestive artwork mural

The Bar-top (The actual bar counter top where you belly up and drinks are placed for you.)

• (-5) Linoleum

<u>Additional</u> (-5) if the linoleum is cracked, split, pieces missing in areas

<u>Additional</u> (-5) if there is a vintage aluminum edge on the linoleum

*Weathered Linoleum, cracked, includes vintage
aluminum edging*

• (-5) Wood Bar-top is well worn and seasoned from years of use, might have cigarette burns, carved initials etc.

Well seasoned bar-top, oh and the cash drawer is left open, (top L corner)

• (-5) Plywood Bar-top

<u>Additional</u> (-10) if the plywood is unfinished, has No polyurethane or other finish, just plain wood

<u>Additional</u> (-10) If you are told *"this is just a temporary top"* but it's been in place for more than a year.

• **+5** (PLUS **5 points**) Cement Bar-top (poured cement bar-top)

• **+5 (plus 5 points)** Copper Bar Top

• **+5** (PLUS **5 points**) Well kept, sturdy wood bar-top, bullnose mahogany for example

• "EPOXY OVER OBJECTS" Bar-top, may or may not indicate a Dive, (use your best judgement.) For example, at seaside locations with seashells and other nautical items encased in epoxy. This one is tough because these bar-tops could determine both Dive or Not depending on the objects encased within the epoxy and also whether the epoxy job was done correctly. These bar-tops can be difficult to make. Many times you will see one that looks like garbage.

APPLY (-5) DIVE POINTS if the objects underneath the epoxy are Nude photos, ridiculous and/or senseless (for example the objects encased are random and have no point or theme) or if the epoxy job is lousy. You can determine this if the epoxy is cloudy or it is sticky in some places because it never cured properly. Often people will carve initials and such into poorly cured epoxy.

ADDITIONAL (-5) IF THERE are dried epoxy drips underneath the edge of the bar-top.

Epoxy drips, dried off bar edge

• **+5 (PLUS 5 points)** If the epoxy job looks good and/or the objects make sense with the bar's theme (for example epoxied seashells at a bar with a seaside theme)

. . .

Dining & Restaurant Considerations

• **+5 (plus 5 points)** Bar has High-Chairs available for children

• **+5 (PLUS 5 points)** Bar has a Kid's Menu

• **+5 (PLUS 5 points)** Bar has crayons and paper for coloring, coloring book, items to entertain children

• **+5 (PLUS 5 points)** Bar has a cocktail menu, Printed menu of elaborate, prepared drinks. Does not include "House Specialty" or drinks that a bar is known for. Apply these points only if the bar has a printed menu of specialty drinks, not on a chalkboard, (printed menus of any kind usually indicates NOT a Dive)

• **+5 (PLUS 5 points)** "Proper Glassware" If you are not sure, skip this one. Basically Non-Dives have different types of glassware while Dives keep things more basic.

Does not include wine glasses but if the bar has on hand ample glassware such as a Rocks glass, Double Rocks glass, Collins glass, Martini/Manhattan stem glass, Snifter Glass etc. then you are probably not at a Dive. Typically staff knows the difference and will use the proper glass for your beverage. Not exactly divey is it, no. However, if the bar makes most of the drinks in pint glasses and has a good quantity of shot glasses then you could be at a Dive.

. . .

• **+20 (PLUS 20 points)** Bar makes Craft Cocktails, Does not include Martini or Manhattan, see definition of Craft Cocktail. If the bartender is shaking you up a Ramos Gin Fizz then most likely you're not at a Dive Bar.

• (-5) BARTENDER CAN MAKE you a Martini or Manhattan but does *not* have the stem glassware, serves these in a Rocks Glass or something other than the proper glass.

• (-5) BARTENDER CANNOT MAKE a Martini or Manhattan, (Bar does not have the ingredients to make these)

• (-10) "REFUSES TO MAKE" Bartender might be able to make a Martini or Manhattan for example but refuses to do this, *"We don't make those here..."*. Surliness should be awarded points. Apply these points if you receive pushback on common requests. Let's be fair on this, if you ask for a Pousse Cafe and they refuse to make it then you are being ridiculous but a more common request like a whiskey sour should be easy enough. Use your best judgement. Don't confuse this with Limited Brands. If you ask for a specific type of vodka and they don't have it, that scenario is handled in the next section. The points here are for surliness not out of stock issues.

• (-5) BAR MAINTAINS an active list of banned customers.
     <u>Additional</u> (-5) List is posted on the wall so that any customer might read the names of the banned individuals.
     <u>Additional</u> (-5) Bar has an "Amnesty Day" where banned customers are allowed back in just for the day. Might be Christmas Day or something like that.

. . .

PRODUCT - WHAT IS SOLD and other things you receive

• (-5) No hot food, no prepared food of any kind sold at this bar. (Free Food offered on Holidays does not affect this. Some Dives have complimentary food for customers such as meatballs in a crock pot on a holiday only)

• (-5) IF A KITCHEN EXISTS but is not used as a kitchen, (Used as an office for example)

• **+10 (PLUS 10 points)** Prepared Hot Food available on a regular basis, cooked by an employee on site.

• **+5 (PLUS 5 points)** Printed Menu, Not on a chalkboard, standard printed menu

• (-5) HOT PREPARED FOOD is available sometimes but only on certain days.

Some days they have food, some days not. If you are told something like, *"Ya we only do food on like Thursday, Friday and Saturday nights I think. It's because the other guy quit and it's just not worth it to do food on the other nights."*

Definitely apply Dive Points in this case.

• (-10) FOOD INCONSISTENCY, This may be difficult to determine but if you hear someone ask the bartender, *"Who's cooking tonight?"* Then you might have additional Dive Points available. If customers prefer one cook's food over another then the food is inconsistent and you should apply Dive Points. Customers might also say things like, *"Oh Billy is on tonight, I'll just get a cheese pizza. Hopefully he won't mess that up."* or, *"Nancy made me a sandwich the other day that was great, Too bad she's not working tonight."* Statements like this indicate inconsistency in the kitchen and might help you determine if you should apply the Dive Points. If you are not sure then skip this one.

Slim Jims for sale, displayed in the original factory box

• (-5) Slim Jims For Sale, Also includes peanuts, potato chips, pretzels, etc. Individual serving size snack bags, Must be for sale, NOT complimentary. If the bartender gives you the snack for free that's ok as long as the snacks are normally for sale. Keep in mind complimentary snacks of any kind means less of a Dive.

Additional (-5): Snack product is displayed in it's own factory "Point of Sale" box.

Therefore Slim Jims for sale, displayed behind the bar in the factory box equals -10 Dive Points. *Oh The Joy!*

Pickled Eggs for sale, photo courtesy of Erin Spaulding

• (-5) Pickled Eggs and/or Pigs Feet for sale, This type of snack food is becoming less common in parts of the country and is awarded extra Dive Points.

• +5 (PLUS **5 points**) Complimentary Snacks, Sometimes called "Bar Mix", Does not include popcorn, If they have the common yellow popcorn from their own machine then skip this. These points are for bars that offer a nicer snack, usually served in small dishes, available to any customer for free. Includes mixed nuts and single serving bags of snack chips, complimentary (not for sale.) Remember complementary is less divey, therefore = **+5**.

• (-5) METAL CHIP RACK sales display

Snack Chips for sale, displayed in the classic metal chip rack

<u>Additional</u> (-5) If Chip Rack has 2 or less bags on display. They have the chip rack but care not to restock the product. This is wonderful and deserves additional Dive Points.

Vintage snack bowls available for use

• (-5) Wooden Snack Bowls, laminated, woven wooden bowls in use for snacks, usually popcorn, peanuts in-shell, etc.

. . .

• (-5) "MYSTERY SHOT" Sold at the bar, also includes Jello shots, (made by the bar in batch quantity and sold for a very affordable price)

Mystery Shot sold with a draft beer combo deal

Additional (-5) if sold in combination with an inexpensive beer. For example, the mystery shot with a draft Pabst Blue Ribbon offered together as a combination, sold at a price you can't refuse.

• (-10) DRAFT BEER TAPS are present but are not in use. Draft system exists but *"It doesn't work,"* or *"We haven't used that in years"* etc.

• (-5) WINE OFFERINGS ARE LIMITED to single serving size bottles. These are typically 187ml, small bottles sometimes called *"Wine Nips."* A truly wonderful offering that almost never satisfies a wine drinker's palette.

• (-10) NO WINE OFFERED at all

· · ·

• (-15) "B̲u̲m̲ W̲i̲n̲e̲" Sold at the bar, these brands include MD 20-20 (Mad Dog), Night Train, Thunderbird, Wild Irish Rose or other fortified flavored wines. An amazing offering worthy of the -15 for sure.

Customer enjoys a wine nip

• (-5) "Limited Offerings" of alcohol brands, (2 or less.) For example, the bar offers 2 or less brands of vodka. Heads Up, there are a ton of potential Dive Points here. If you ask for Absolut but the only vodka available is a brand you are not familiar with, by all means, apply the Dive Points.

• Additional (-5) For each category of alcohol that is limited. For example, the bar has Well Level Whiskey and Jack Daniels but that's it for whiskey, apply additional points. Categories are: Vodka, Gin, Rum, Whiskey, Tequila (total of -25 Dive Points available)

. . .

For Clarification: If the bar carries 2 or less brands on a regular basis, that is Limited Offerings. If you are told, *"Sorry we are out of that right now..."* this means they might get more in tomorrow. It is important to pay attention to what the bar usually carries day to day. They might normally carry 8 different brands and you happened to be there right before delivery. However, if the bar normally has no gin, no tequila, only one type of vodka, rum and whiskey then hey, -25 it is.

• (-5) Limited or No Garnishes for drinks, For example they might only have a lime wedge but that's it, no other fruits garnishes, no cherries, no olives, etc. If you ask for a lime and the bartender needs to cut you a wedge or leave the bar to go get one, it means they don't normally do the lime thing. Dive Bars tend not to bother with a lot of fruit.

• (-5) Lottery Sold at the bar, Could be any state sponsored lottery game, Keno, scratch tickets etc.

• +5 (plus 5 points) Cocktails on Draft, Drinks made in batch quantity and served from the draft system does not indicate you are at a Dive.

• +5 (plus 5 points) High number of Draft Lines, 12 or more draft lines in use.

Singularities

(-15) One Singularity, (maximum of -45 points or 3 Singularities per bar.) Covered in Chapter 6, Please familiarize yourself with the details regarding Singularities. These unique or rare oddities could include aspects about the building that are strange or unorthodox and might also be a person associated with the bar that is very unique. They help affirm you are at a Dive.

*Taxidermy at it's finest, a good example of beyond eclectic,
a one of a kind, Singularity.*

Restrooms

• (-5) Small Restrooms, especially one-at-a-time size

If the restroom is small but nice, smells clean, well maintained, then skip this.

• (-5) "ODD RESTROOM AWKWARDNESS" Awkward doorway, broken latch, unlockable, no door at all, not handicap accessible etc. Example: One needs to go behind the bar to access the restroom or confined space, not enough room to open the stall door if someone is at the urinal, etc.

Broken restroom door latch

• (-5) "Unconventional Plumbing" Includes Self-closing flusher handles, These valves are functional but not originally intended for use as a flush valve but hey, they do the trick. Apply Dive Points.

Completely serviceable yet leans towards the "Gas Station" kind of experience

• (-5) BROKEN PORCELAIN FIXTURES

Additional (-5) if repaired with construction adhesive. Therefore a sink, toilet, or urinal that was broken and is now glued back together equals -10 Dive points... nice.

• (-20) TROUGH URINAL, A restroom Holy Grail find, becoming more rare all the time, deserved Dive Points for sure.

• (-15) "CONTINUOUS FEED" A rare type of towel dispenser, even if empty, a beautiful find for sure.

"Continuous Feed" Towel dispenser

• (-5) EMPTY PAPER TOWEL AND/OR hand soap dispenser in restroom

• (-5) BUSTED TOWEL DISPENSER or a place on the wall where the dispenser used to be.

Additional (-5) If paper towel roll is on or near the sink, sitting in a puddle.

• (-10) INCREDIBLE AMOUNTS OF GRAFFITI. Every restroom has some graffiti, this needs to be a lot, as in all 4 walls or more. (see photo of Snake & Jakes in Chapter 5 regarding Restrooms)

Restroom door spring shenanigans

• (-5) Restroom Shenanigans, this is humorous graffiti or other nonsense you might find in a restroom. It's half the graffiti points than above but awards points for small amounts of stupid creativity.

• **+10** (PLUS **10 points**) Air Freshener, of any kind, spray, solid, whatever is NOT divey so + 10 points.

• (-15) EVIDENCE OF ILLICIT BEHAVIOR, lines of coke left on the back of the toilet, Drug paraphernalia and the like.

• (-15) MULTIPLE PEOPLE ENTERING a restroom intended for single person use.

. . .

PATRON ACTIVITIES (these are events you might witness while at the bar)

• (-5) A CUSTOMER IS SHUT-OFF (refused service)

• (-10) A CUSTOMER IS THROWN OUT, (physically removed for the barroom)

• (-5) A CUSTOMER SPEAKS to you with unintelligible words. Must be someone you do not know, the person tries to communicate with you in a garbled, unintelligible way.

• (-15) A FIRE BREAKS OUT, Includes Electrical fires and doesn't necessarily mean anyone will call the Fire Department.

Smoky barroom, not due to cigarette or other patron activities

Additional (-10) If no one leaves their barstool during the fire event.

• (-5) A CUSTOMER PRODUCES audible flatulence

• (-10) A CUSTOMER REMOVES dentures (for any reason) or if the teeth fall out or are blatantly adjusted in plain sight, perhaps a glorious display for fellow patrons

• (-5) CUSTOMERS AND/OR Staff are having a public conversation with a negative tone about Divorce, Ex-Lover, Old relationship bitterness, etc. Must be a negative, bitter discourse.

•   •   •

• (-5) YAHTZEE OR DICE ROLL, Must be for money, Customers try to roll 5 of a kind dice. Typically a small bet ($2 maybe), rules vary house to house but this is considered petty gambling and usually frowned upon by the authorities. Boo authorities.

• (-5) CUSTOMER DELIBERATELY BREAKS A GLASS. Whatever method is used but must not be accidental.

• (-10) "RAW MEAT TRANSACTION" A customer buys, sells or gives raw meat of any kind to a fellow patron, (includes seafood.) This is a Customer to Customer transaction where they meet for a drink at the bar and make the exchange. The bar is just the meeting place and is not involved with the transaction itself. This also counts if the actual transfer of raw meat is outside the bar (parking lot etc.) as long as one person involved is an active customer of the bar at the time.

Cooler of fresh Gulf Shrimp waiting for the buyer to arrive at the bar, while the Shrimp Boat Capt. has a cold beer

Examples: *"Ya I'm just havin' a drink, waiting for Marc, he's bringing me over a cooler of shrimp"*

or

"Bobby is gonna stop by with some lobsta faw me"

or

"Mike shot a nice buck the other day, he's bringing some down now"

or

"I'm tellin' you, this is good stuff, you gotta take some"

PUKING or Otherwise

• (-5) A CUSTOMER GETS UP and runs to the restroom in desperate haste

TED MAGUIRE

(we don't need to know why)

- (-5) A CUSTOMER THROWS-UP into a trash barrel, at the end of the bar for example.
  <u>Additional</u> (-5) Misses the barrel

- (-5) A CUSTOMER hastily runs outside to throw-up
  <u>Additional</u> (-10) Doesn't make it outside

- (-15) A CUSTOMER just outright throws-up inside the bar, seated or standing. Makes no attempt to save face.
  <u>Additional</u> (-10) If the customer is allowed to remain drinking in the bar after any of the above puke incidents.

ALL INCIDENTS/ACTIVITIES listed above need to happen organically in order to collect points. The customer(s) in question cannot be associated with you. For example, if your friend farts loudly inside and proceeds to puke all over himself you cannot apply Dive points for your friend's actions. Please feel free to deal with your friend accordingly aside from your Dive assessment.

Photo Exercise Answer Key

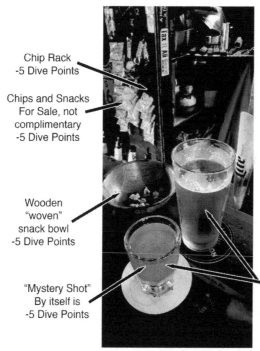

Chip Rack
-5 Dive Points

Chips and Snacks
For Sale, not
complimentary
-5 Dive Points

Wooden
"woven"
snack bowl
-5 Dive Points

"Mystery Shot"
By itself is
-5 Dive Points

"Mystery Shot"
Sold as a combo with
inexpensive draft
(usually considered
a house special offer)
add an additional
-5 Dive Points

Total of -25 Dive Points with potentially -15 more by way of a Sticker
Collection, Worn Bar-top and a Kitchen not used as a kitchen.
Difficult to tell by a photograph alone but you get the concept.

MAGUIRE'S DIVE CHART
Total 'er up Barkeep

NEXT STEP: Total the Dive Points accumulated by the bar you're assessing. Hopefully you have a nice big Negative Number. Compare the bar's total on the Dive Chart to see where it ranks. A positive number means NOT a Dive while a negative number means DIVE BAR. The Dive Chart further breaks down more precisely how divey your Dive really is.

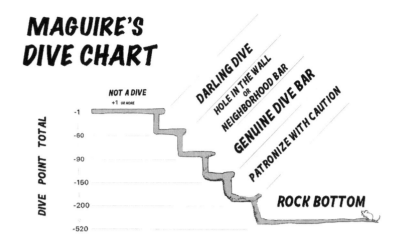

MAGUIRE'S DIVE CHART

+1 or Higher is NOT A DIVE

-1 to -59, "Darling Dive"

Still a Dive Bar but something is askew here. Some argue this bar is not a Dive at all. This level of Dive might have great food or something that keeps the bar from achieving a more impressive Dive Level. A bar at this status is operating in tepid waters and might consider going in one direction or another. Make a few improvements and become a nice little restaurant OR hang up a Velvet Elvis and let the dust settle. Offer some Slim Jims maybe, become more like that Hole in the Wall you thought you were.

-60 to - 89, "Hole in the Wall" or "Neighborhood Bar"

Many bars fall into this category. They typically serve the local area within a few blocks around them. They are the comfortable old sweater type of place where you meet friends without even texting a plan. Regulars and Staff know each other like old friends. These bars are usually in place for decades and provide a kind of service for their community. This level confuses a lot of people because frankly they haven't read this book. They might take a second to think about the difference between the "Hole in the Wall" and their favorite Mom & Pop restaurant... Jackwagons.

-90 to -149, "Genuine Dive Bar"

Now we're talking. Your favorite Dives will most likely fall into this category. This bar has enough Dive Points to Qualify as a Dive in most anyone's opinion. People sometimes keep these locations a secret unless they know you well enough. This level never disappoints. As a Dive appreciateur you feel at home, no doubt you have arrived. You might only complete an assessment just to see how divey your fav place actually is.

-150 to -199, "Patronize with Caution"

A Dive Bar scoring in this range on Maguire's Dive Chart is considered fairly divey and may not be so friendly. An unfamiliar face might be met with suspicion. Too late! You've already entered, can't turn back now. As a first time customer, your best move is to keep it simple, don't order anything that requires a lot of steps or is not recognized as a common beverage. Once you are there long enough, you can assess whether it's safe to order your *"Pineapple Rumtastic with an umbrella,"* nonsense that, for the love of Pete, you cannot stop ordering. Unless the bar is known for a specialty rum drink then your best bet is to keep it simple. Basic bottled beer, rum and coke, whiskey and ginger or just ...whiskey. Dive Bars keep it simple, you should too. After all, why make your Dive experience difficult because you just had to have blue cheese stuffed olives in your slightly dirty, Chopin vodka martini with rocks on the side. If a bartender abruptly points at you and then points at the door, you own that. This level of Dive can be amazing but the caution statement is there because you might need to employ a little more street smarts. This will be down and dirty drinking like there's no tomorrow except the bar will be open early tomorrow if you need more. You may also witness some illicit activity. It is not recommended to get involved with that, patronize with caution anyhow.

-200 OR MORE, "ROCK BOTTOM"

Well, we're here. This level is tough to earn. No doubt a lot of insane, crazy nonsense has helped to score the bar at this level. Hopefully not too much bloodshed. Employ as much street smarts as possible if you choose to patronize on a regular basis. Interestingly, a bar at this level might be on it's way out. Owners/Managers will either reel things in or sell. If you are looking to buy a Dive Bar this might be your chance. If you have the opportunity to buy something like this, the suggestion is to eliminate only enough bad aspects so that you maintain some-where in the -90 to -199 on Maguire's Dive Chart. It will not be easy to accomplish but you will earn the great distinction as someone who saved a Dive Bar. That alone is worth a lifetime of effort.

IF YOU WOULD LIKE to contribute your assessment results to the grand Dive data bank, please do so at:
www.DiveBarBook.com

9

SOME FINAL THOUGHTS

*"After being at the bar I feel great. My problems aren't
nearly as bad as the people I was just hangin' with"*

THE DOSE OF SOLID REALITY WE EXPERIENCE IN A DOWN TO
Earth environment where everyone is equal can be found but a
Dive serves it up with superior presentation and in substantial
helpings. A vast improvement over other sources for sure. The

Dive Bar satisfies a need in all of us to be grounded, balanced, and well hydrated. Dives are often thought of as a place to avoid even though every patron is there by their own volition. Just being present says something about you. While some may scoff, you have thrown caution to the wind. You could care less how others may judge. It's a way to be yourself and release some of life's weight even if temporarily. We are naturally social and cannot change that. Dive Bars provide a complex variety of solutions for problems we are not even aware we have or want to think about. The dirtiest, most insane Dive might have a soft side that can be therapeutic. A side that reassures, *"You're fine, you're gonna make it."* You may never want to get to know this side of your favorite bar. You don't want to think about it in a caring, soft way and that's fine but if Robbie is drunk (again) and needs a ride home, don't hesitate to help. No one will claim you're soft for doing that.

"Where did my bar go to"

AT SOME POINT you might experience "Dive Acclimation." It's a condition to be aware of. Once you are a regular, the bar becomes less of a Dive and essentially more like your average bar. "Surly Bob" is now your friend and his surliness is just his style and you love the undying, curmudgeonly attitude. You no longer see the dirt. The quirky oddness becomes part of the background, invisible, just part of your home. Your Dive becomes your house. The regulars are now family. Do Not Fear, suffering from Dive Acclimation is a natural progression. If you have concerns, there are a number of actions to take. The easiest solution is to look at some old photos of your bar when you first met. Remind yourself of the original feelings and impressions. You might also show someone a picture from that time. Their recollections might spark some fond memories of the filth you have forgotten. Stories about incidents of insanity are always good to help remind you that your Dive is alive and well.

"REMEMBER when Frank put those storage shelves up all lousy and the next day they collapsed, sending cartons of popcorn and snacks all over the couple sitting there, I mean the guy didn't even move, he just sat there with stuff falling on him. And then Frank was like, hey you gotta move, didn't even buy him a drink or anything. I would have at least bought them a drink ya know like, I mean Frank must have been pretty drunk when he installed those shelves."

Word to the wise, listening to stories like this requires that you do some listening, so be sure the individual you're talking with has a shut-off valve before you commence your therapy session. Too much will not be helpful. It's similar to eating chocolates, delicious until you over do it. Generally though, Dive Acclimation is never a bad thing as long as you always keep sight of why you loved the bar in the first place.

THERE ARE places where pretty much every bar is a dive. Yes, it's utopian for sure but if every bar is a Dive then there is no frame of reference. We recognise a Dive Bar because the nice restaurant has provided you with that. You experienced nice, so when you enter the Dive you have an educated view. The bigger the difference, the more divey the bar might seem. So now when you enter this Utopia place everything has shifted in the direction of divey. The least divey bar is now the fancy bar and so on. In places like this the locals might become agitated if you ask for information about Dives in the area. They may not even know what the term Dive Bar means. When you attempt to describe a Dive you are met with, *"What do you mean, all our bars are like that..."* Remember, they don't mean to be divey, they just naturally created amazing bars. A real Dive happens organically over time, not deliberately created. Be careful not to insult the locals wherever you visit and remember Heavy Tipping makes up for most transgressions. This is never something you should test, just keep it in mind. The general idea is to be welcomed back. Bartenders see all and remember nothing unless the tip is lousy. In which case, the memory becomes indelible. It's an unintentional consequence of being in the service industry.

WITH JOY and dedication similar to neighborhood kids chasing down the Ice Cream Truck, you must patronize your Dives. The number of them out there can be fleeting. Some will close permanently before you bear witness to their brilliance and grandeur. Sure you can continue patronizing your favorite chain, they have their place, but a Dive can definitely be considered a better option. One cannot put this off. You must make it happen today and continue it as a lifestyle. There is a magnificent slice of life waiting for you at a Dive Bar.

ACKNOWLEDGMENTS

My daughter Pamela for her artwork, illustrations, advice and support. More illustrations @pamlikesyou

Jeff Davidson, known to some as "Canal Jeff", who corroborated my opinions regarding Dive Bars and wrote down some notes during his shift, bartending one night. These notes became the initial basis for the qualification system presented in this book.

Much thanks to Robin O'Brien for pointing out the particulars on punctuation, especially the use of a comma after the word: However.

The friends and acquaintances who have joined me regularly out there for a cool, refreshing beverage. I look forward to the next meeting.

GLOSSARY OF TERMS

Back-up: This is the drink you order when you cannot get your "Go To"

Occasionally your "Go To" is not available, you simply switch to the Back-up and you're good. Some people have a number of these at the ready. It is highly recommended that you remember this anytime you are ordering drinks especially when the bar is busy.

Craft Cocktail: A drink NOT available at Dive Bars. Includes Prohibition Era, multi step procedure, ingredients not widely available, typically priced above average, etc.

Examples include the Sazerac, Old Fashioned, Negroni, French 75, Moscow Mule (especially if served in a copper mug), Mojito, Ramos Gin Fizz, Muddled anything, Organic ingredients, Barrel Aged, Drinks with Bitters especially if the Bitters is other than Angostura.

IMPORTANT: Martinis and Manhattans are often lumped in with the Craft Cocktail group. These may or may not fall into the "Craft Cocktail" category. Ingredients used when making them are an important consideration.

Dive Acclimation: A condition that occurs when an individual has become a frequent enough customer that the Divey aspects of the bar seem to fade. The individual feels a sense of loss and regret. This view of their favorite bar can develop over time and is a normal progression which is treatable by conjuring the memories of when they first walked in as a new customer.

Dive Appreciateur: Someone who appreciates Dive Bars and includes them as part of their lifestyle. This individual also knows that outside judgements, labels and discussions about changing their lifestyle are entirely unnecessary. Thank you very much.

Dive Ethics: The unwritten code of behavior that everyone should follow. No one should act like or want to be the Jackwagon.

Dive Bar: A wonderment to behold, The name awarded to an establishment that has scored low enough to qualify for this title. Also described as "A community of intemperate personalities, acting subtly disobedient while self medicating in a location which many view as downright filthy or worse."

Dive Level: A specific level that a bar might achieve using Maguire's Dive Bar Qualifier system.

Dive Points: These are values (listed on Maguire's Dive Points List) given to the various aspects and nuances about a bar. These points ultimately determine a bar's Dive Level.

Dive Professional (or Dive Bar Professional): Someone who gets it, the opposite of a Jackwagon.

Dive Status: A level which is earned and should be admired.

Dive Wonderment: Anything in or about a Dive Bar that makes you feel a sense of joy and helps you strive to be a better person overall and keep on keeping on.

Drink: Liquid beverage, may or **may not** be alcoholic. If a bartender asks, *"What can I get you"*, DO NOT assume they mean alcoholic beverage, they just want to put a glass of something in your hand. If you don't want one, it is your responsibility to politely tell the bartender, *"I'm all set, thanks"* or something of this nature.

Genuine Dive (or Genuine Dive Bar): A specific level described on Maguire's Dive Chart earned by a bar with numerous and indisputable Dive Points. The Dive Status is clear and obvious.

Go To: This is the drink you typically order and enjoy on a regular basis. You might be known by this drink. If someone buys this for you, it is ALWAYS acceptable to you even if you did not ask for it. This drink will never let you down.

Healthy Dive: A situation whereby the Owner, Staff and Customers of a Dive Bar are unknowingly working in unison and have created a wonderment to behold.

Jackwagon: A person you should not aspire to be nor hangout with. This individual might be clueless and/or annoying to say the least.

Maguire's Dive Chart: Contained in this book, the chart displays specific Dive Status levels earned after careful consideration and assessment is made. The chart helps to determine more precisely how the establishment is considered. A total score in the negative indicates Dive while a positive score indicates Not a Dive.

Maguire's Dive Points List: Contained in this book, a list of attributes and their corresponding values. The list becomes the tool by which a Dive Status is determined. This list should not be used while inside any bar.

Maguire's Dive Bar Qualification System: A fair and reasonable process to determine whether or not a bar can be awarded Dive Status. This system employs the use of tools, such as but not limited to, Maguire's Dive Points List, Maguire's Dive Chart, the general information contained within chapters of this book as well as the keen eye of the Dive Appreciateur.

Mystery Shot: A house drink available at most Dive Bars, mixed in batch quantity, served in a shot glass. They are a fun, inexpensive way for customers to have a shot and it's a great way for the house to use up the bottles that aren't selling or use up free promotional bottles. The recipe might change often, hence the mystery. The drink usually looks and tastes similar to whatever powdered drink mix was used in the recipe, orange, grape, cherry, etc. Refreshing and Delicious.

Nationally Recognized Beer: The definition should be obvious but these are beer brands that are widely available, and NOT a Craft Beer. They come in handy as a "Back-up Beverage" or for many they are the "Go To." Brands include beers from Anheuser Busch, Coors, Miller among others. They help keep things simple and might be useful in certain situations.

Quiet Paper Reading Time: (a phrase coined by Peter Enos) This happens whenever a regular is sitting alone at the bar, reading something quietly to themselves, usually a newspaper but could be anything. It is wise not to disturb this person in any manner. Quiet Paper Reading Time should be quiet, hardly a time for idle chatter.

Regular(s): These are customers of the bar that return often. Much can be learned from them either directly or just observing, listening etc.

Shifties: Drinks consumed by the staff at the end of their shift. Staff at some bars are allowed one complimentary drink at the end of their shift. The rules on this are often stretched.

Support Business: A retail business located very near a Dive Bar which sells products not available from the bar itself. They provide the bar's customers with items required for daily survival and betterment. These products include but are not limited to Tobacco, Lottery, Pizza, Sandwiches, Sundries and the like.

That Guy: A person you should not aspire to be and is most likely a Jackwagon.

Well Level: This is the least expensive brand of alcohol available in a bar. Some refer to this as "Bar level." For example, *"I'll have a Bloody Mary, Well Vodka is fine,"* meaning they don't want the expensive stuff.

Any names used in this book for examples and anecdotal stories have been changed to protect the innocent.

Do not drink like an idiot. Please keep yourself together. If other people end up having to take care of you then you have become a problem. Don't do that. Everyone has a night where things go wrong, keep that to an absolute minimum, maybe never.

Call a cab, Uber, Lyft, a friend or just walk but do not drive under the influence. If you cannot do this then alcohol is not for you. There are no exceptions.

Peace & Love